THE SABBATH

C. H. Pappas ThM

WESTBOW
P R E S S®
A DIVISION OF THOMAS NELSON
& ZONDERVAN

KJV: Scripture taken from the King James Version of the Bible.

WestBow Press books may be ordered through booksellers or by contacting:

WestBow Press
A Division of Thomas Nelson & Zondervan
1663 Liberty Drive
Bloomington, IN 47403
www.westbowpress.com
1 (866) 928-1240

ISBN: 978-1-9736-0416-7 (sc)
ISBN: 978-1-9736-0415-0 (hc)
ISBN: 978-1-9736-0417-4 (e)

Library of Congress Control Number: 2017915366

Print information available on the last page.

WestBow Press rev. date: 07/10/2018

Dedicated to the Saints at Collins Road Baptist Church:
A Lily among the Thorns

I wish to express my sincere thanks to
Travis & Amelia Crane for their labor in editing.

CONTENTS

INTRODUCTION

It may seem strange to the reader that one would address the doctrine of the Sabbath. This is especially true in that it appears that there are weightier matters at hand. One would think the doctrine of the Sabbath would be the least of those things that should be addressed in such times as these. The church has fallen into a miserable state, and the nation is about to collapse. Although this is true, nothing is more needful in this hour than a proper understanding of the fourth commandment. Unless we come to a proper understanding of the Sabbath, none of the problems with which we are faced will be solved.

I am aware that this may seem strange falling upon the ears of this generation as the fourth commandment is regarded with little or no value. For the most part it is ignored. With the exception of a few, no one heeds the injunction of the fourth commandment. As for those who do observe the Sabbath, they are a small remnant, and their number is growing smaller with each passing day.

Maybe this is because the fourth commandment has long been ignored. Or it could be that it is assumed to some degree that it is understood, and therefore there is no need to exhort men to observe the Sabbath. But this is not likely. As for myself, for more than half of a century of my Christian life, I had never heard a single message addressing the imperativeness of Sabbath observance. This is not to imply that no one had ever addressed the subject. But as for myself,

I had never heard a single message from the pulpit or on the radio admonishing people to "Remember the Sabbath day, to keep it holy." I have heard, "You need to be in church on Sunday!" But this too was seldom.

This is even more pronounced when, from the time of my conversion, I had never missed a church service with the exception of providential hindrances, such as sickness, and that was very seldom. Other than that, I attended Bible conferences, revival meetings and Bible seminars. Is this not telling? All of this indicates that the fourth commandment has been ignored by Christendom, as a whole, for a very long time.

What is also arresting is that there are many Christian books on the market touching upon many Biblical subjects, but nothing can be found addressing the fourth commandment. In perusing through books in Christian bookstores, I cannot find a single book addressing the fourth commandment. This is arresting. Can you, dear reader, remember the last time you were exhorted to observe the Sabbath day to keep it holy? How long has it been since you have heard such an exhortation? Is it not frightening that the pulpits in America, as a whole, are silent when it comes to such a grave matter as this? Is it any wonder that professing Christendom has come to think that the fourth commandment is either non-essential or, in some way, has become obsolete? Some are confused asking, "How many commandments are there—nine or ten?"

Being converted at the age of twenty-six, I was seized by the wonder and marvel of the love of God. It was altogether staggering how God, through His free grace and mercy, saves sinners, especially one like me. I esteemed everything else to be less than dung in light of the glorious message of the Gospel of our Lord Jesus Christ. From that day, there was but one objective, and that was to come to know the Master better and lead men to a saving knowledge of our Lord Jesus Christ. All the exhortations coming from the pulpit were, in essence, to repent and believe on the Lord Jesus Christ, in which I rejoiced. However, very little was said concerning how we should then live. When it came to observing the Sabbath, there was frightening silence.

Why this strange phenomenon? As for the Ten Commandments, nine are, without question, binding. These come as trumpet blasts at times from our pulpits. But the fourth commandment somehow lies dormant. When it is brought into question, it is said to be more or less ceremonial. Thus, the fourth commandment is not taken seriously, even though all commerce, at one time, came to a halt, and the nation, in general, went up to the house of the LORD to worship. From all appearances, it seemed as if the fourth commandment, in some respects, was observed. At least this was the impression given. But things began to change in the 1960's. Presently, we are experiencing a great falling away. A great cloud shadows the land as none of the commandments are taken seriously. What has happened?

Although I was an Isaac, I was more like an Ishmael wandering through a maze seeking light and gradually coming into it. The light I received was questioned by my spiritual guides. However, it was understood that we were to come up to the house of the Lord on the Lord's Day. This was never in question. As for the reasons given in seminary when the subject came up, and that was very seldom, the views of the Reformers were briefly cited. Our professors told us that the Reformers were divided on the subject. No concretes were given as professors sought to avoid the subject. They left each student to work it out according to the individual's conscience. Thus, the fourth commandment had become subjective and, in most cases, lay dormant.

The pervading thought of our day is that the fourth commandment is not something upon which to build a society. It has no moral value or ethical relevance of one's conduct towards others, or for that matter, in society at large. However, if one does not even believe in Jehovah, then the first four commandments are meaningless. Furthermore, some think that the fifth commandment has little or no value as it only pertains to parents and children, and the last five commandments are presently viewed by contemporaries as having little moral relevance. Hence, Christians are left to fend for themselves in this religious maze. Divorced from concretes, many are left to their feelings to work things out, which are the most unstable thing concerning man.

It is frightening how far the Church of our Lord Jesus Christ has fallen. Some may be familiar with a 1924 Olympian, Eric Liddell. Liddell announced to his country that he would not run the 100-meter sprint because the finals were scheduled to be held on a Sunday. He had labored hard for this moment, and now that it had finally arrived, he refused to run. He was the fastest human alive, but he was going to forgo that honor. Sunday was the Lord's Day, a day of worship and rest for Eric Liddell. He would not run even if he were the only hope of winning an Olympic gold medal for his beloved country, Scotland.

The people of Scotland became very angry. Even though all commerce stopped, and all labor ceased on the Sabbath at the time (that is in America), the papers still wrote scathing reports about him. Some people even called him a traitor. Their hero had become a Judas in their eyes. They heaped one criticism after another upon him. He who was loved was now despised. This no doubt weighed heavily upon him. He had horrendous pressure coming from every direction to get him to change his mind. After all, the race would last no more than ten seconds! Just to take a few minutes of the Sabbath day to run; surely the Lord would not care.

His own teammates did what they could to persuade him to run as well. Surely the Lord would understand! But Liddell stood firm. He never ran on the Sabbath and he never would, not even for an Olympic gold medal. He realized the seriousness of being a Sabbath breaker, even though the world around him thought otherwise. He was not about to allow the world to influence him. He was determined to honor the Lord regardless of the cost. He also realized what a great sin it would be to fail to observe the Sabbath. Thus, Harold Abraham, whom he had beaten in an earlier race by a considerable distance, ran and won the gold.

Then Liddell was scheduled to run the 400 meter, an event he was not supposed to win. There were two Americans who held world record times, and either of the two was expected to win the gold. Eric Liddell was not even expected to place. However, just before the race, a man slipped a note in Liddell's pocket. It read, "They that honor God, God will honor."

The gun went off! They were running! When he came to the 220-meter mark, his time was remarkably fast. His trainers were concerned that he would not have enough strength to finish. They thought he was running too fast and would not last. Then Liddell came to the last turn and found himself alone. His strength did not diminish. He pressed for the finish line and won! It was a marvel; it was an upset! He had stunned the world. He won the gold. He also had set a world record!

His nation that hated him now loved him. The papers that maligned him were now going all out to lavish praises upon him. He who was earlier despised and called a Judas had now become their nation's hero. But Eric Liddell did not seek the praises of men but rather the praise that only comes from God. He said he ran the first 100 meters, and God ran the final 300 meters.

Liddell returned to China where His parents were missionaries. He was there when the Japanese conquered China. They took him captive and placed him in a concentration camp. There he labored, going out each day ministering to his fellow prisoners. One morning he could not get up. He could not move. He had a brain tumor and shortly thereafter, he died. His beloved Scotland mourned His death. His legacy from his own mouth was that God made him run fast to defend the Sabbath.

How different is this than that which we are presently witnessing. Professing "Christian" athletes are on the field playing ball on the Sabbath and think nothing of it. Neither do pastors and evangelists think anything of it as they are not hesitant to invite athletes to stand in their pulpits and give their testimonies of their relationship with Christ.

Adding to this confusion, professing Christians sit in the bleachers or in their living rooms watching the games on their televisions on the Sabbath. And if it is Super Bowl Sunday, a big screen TV is set up in the Church so that the congregation may watch the game. Can it be that we have failed to realize the seriousness of being Sabbath breakers? How have we become insensitive to our declension? What does it mean to "Remember the Sabbath day, to keep it holy"?

> Oh how gradually we fall away, Unconscious of
> our own decay! In our pride we think that all is
> well, While treading on the road to hell.

> Shall we not obey our God,
> He hath showered us with love!
> Oh let us from our heart obey,
> And Sanctify the Sabbath day.

CHAPTER 1

Sabbath Breaking is a Serious Crime

It is frightening how one can commit a serious crime and at the same time be insensitive to it. This is the condition of serial killers. Have we in some respects become like them? Consider how the unacceptable has gradually become accepted. People have forgotten how to blush. Not only has the unthinkable become the norm, crying out against such crimes as abortion and homosexuality will only bring the anathemas of the public upon our heads. We should be struck with horror as the unthinkable has become the rule. How have we become so desensitized to evil? The common denominator that reduces us all to pagans is irreverence!

It is apparent that the conscience of the nation is seared. The church, in some respects, has become conditioned by the world. After all, consider how many professing Christians profane the Sabbath without their conscience being pricked! At least this is true with the majority of professing Christendom. On the other hand, those who strive to keep the Sabbath day holy are seen as legalists, if not extremists. They are said to be "over the top." Why is this? How did we ever come to embrace such thinking? It is apparent that the unthinkable has not remained unthinkable!

1

In order to have a proper respect for the Sabbath, some consideration should be given to that which is recorded in Numbers Chapter 15. There we read of a certain man who was arrested and later executed. His crime was gathering sticks on the Sabbath. To most this seems to be beyond the pale. This would be true if the observance of the Sabbath is only a mere ritual. However, this is not the case. If it were a mere ritual, then why did God command that this person be put to death? All he did was gather a few sticks on the Sabbath day. Do we not do much worse?

We should also keep in mind that only those guilty of a capital crime were to be put to death. From what is revealed in this 15th chapter of Numbers, failure to keep the Sabbath day holy is a very serious offense. It is a capital crime. If this were not the case, then why was this man put to death? We know that our God is a merciful God having no pleasure in the death of the wicked (Ezekiel 33:11). Yet it was He Who had passed this awful sentence upon this Sabbath breaker. When Moses inquired of the LORD what to do with him, our Lord said, "STONE HIM!"

Christians, in some strange way, have become desensitized to this sin. In reading this narrative, in our minds we inquire, "What great crime is there in gathering a few sticks on the Sabbath?" Gathering a few sticks on the Sabbath day does not seem to be a crime much less an offense worthy of death. This is especially true in that we are guilty of much worse. Does this mean we too are subjects of Divine displeasure? Remember, God is no respecter of persons.

What is of further interest is that this man was not only to be put to death, but his execution was not to take place in some remote area out of the sight of the people. Instead, God commanded that the entire congregation should witness the stoning of this man. We can imagine this was no pleasant sight, yet the congregation did as God commanded. They witnessed the execution of this man who gathered a few sticks on the Sabbath. Is this not sobering? Neither was the offender turned over to an executioner to carry out this dreadful sentence.

In this case, the people were not only to witness the execution; they were also to be the executioners. The congregation was to take up stones and stone the Sabbath breaker unto death. It is one thing to witness an execution, but it is another to be the executioner. Our Lord had the congregation cast stones until this man was dead. Why was this mandated? Was it not to further impress upon their minds the dreadfulness of profaning the Sabbath? Was it not to instill fear in the hearts of the people in order that they would "Remember the Sabbath day, to keep it holy"?

At one time in this country, executions were public. People were hung in the public square. An elderly man once shared with me how his father had taken him to witness a public hanging when he was but a child. After the offender was executed, he said that his father looked him in his eyes and said, "Son, this is what they do with wicked people." He said he never forgot it. It made a deep impression upon his mind to obey the Law. Was this not the impression our Lord desired to impress upon the minds of those who witnessed this man's execution?

Some may be of the opinion that such a penalty in failing to observe the Sabbath was much too severe. It appears that the punishment exceeded the offense. Then there are some who dismiss what is said altogether, thinking that it was just the Old Testament which is not relevant to us today. Is this true or have we become so hardened to sin that sin has become tolerable if not acceptable? It would be good to consider some of the laws legislated against Sabbath breakers in early America.

For an example, one of the laws legislated was as follows:

Whosoever shall profane the Lords-day, or any part of it, either by sinful servile work, or by unlawful sport, recreation or otherwise, whether wilfully or in a careless neglect, shall be duly punished by fine, imprisonment, or corporally, according to the nature, and measure of the sinn, and offence. But if the court upon examination, by clear, and satisfying evidence find that the sin was proudly, presumptuously, and with a high hand committed against the known command and authority of the blessed God, such a person therein despising and reproaching the Lord, shall be put to death, that all others may feare and shun such provoking rebellious courses.[1]

In early America, if one had no regard for the Sabbath, it was considered a capital offense. Those in authority did not hesitate to put Sabbath breakers to death if they proudly sinned. Nor did authorities hesitate to deny Sabbath breakers their provisions for the coming week as well as being publically whipped if they had carelessly stumbled. Many years later, in the early 1830s, these laws were somewhat relaxed. Alexis de Tocqueville, who visited America at this time, writes,

Although the puritanical strictness that presides at the birth of the English colonies in America had greatly relaxed, extraordinary traces of it remained in habit and in law. [2]

People were no longer executed for breaking the Sabbath, but fines were imposed upon those who had their shops open or if any were recreating on the Sabbath day. The Sabbath was to be strictly observed. Early America understood that it was imperative that the fourth commandment was to be observed. She understood that her existence depended upon a consciousness of God by which she was governed.

---

[1] William Addison Blakely, *American State Papers Bearing on Sunday Legislation* (Washington D.C.: The Religious Liberty Association, 1911), 42.
[2] Alexis de Tocqueville, *Democracy in America* (New York: The Library of America, 2004), 839.

In time, there were further relaxations as officials no longer imposed fines upon those who failed to observe the Sabbath. Nevertheless, Sabbath breakers were looked upon with disdain. Public sentiment had not yet changed since people were still outraged if a neighbor hung her wash on the line or if one cut his lawn on the Sabbath. All shops remained closed on the Sabbath and the streets, for the most part, were deserted. But as darkness stealthily came over the land, all the blue laws were removed and the Sabbath was no longer revered. The church had failed to stay the corruption.

Griffith's biography of John Bunyan sheds an interesting light on Bunyan's Sabbath activities before his conversion. He tells how he went to church twice on Sunday and thought himself free to do what he would thereafter. Thus after dinner, he went with the youth to play a game they called tip-cat. He struck the peg with a fair blow. Then when he was about to strike the peg again, he was suddenly struck with horrible conviction. He was a Sabbath breaker! He rose up and stood thinking he was going to hell. He had that very day heard a thunderous sermon of God's wrath poured out on Sabbath breakers. He thought to shrug it off, but God seized him and he knew he was going to hell. Later we know of his conversion. From thence, he faithfully hallowed the Sabbath.[3]

This is relevant because there are many who esteem the Tinker highly but fail to appreciate his reverence for the Sabbath. He understood that Sabbath breakers were damned to hell. Thus when he realized he had committed such a horrible crime in the middle of his play, he froze. He was guilty of a capital crime. This was never opened for debate. It was understood that Sabbath breakers were guilty of committing a very grievous sin worthy of eternal damnation.

---

[3] William O. Griffith, *John Bunyan* (London: Hodder and Stoughton, 1927), 72.

How have we become so desensitized to such a horrid offense? What has happened to the Church? She is the light of the world. How did she lose her light! How has she become oblivious to her wounds? The spirit of the world has influenced the Church instead of the Spirit of the Church influencing the world. O how the mighty have fallen!

The consequences of Sabbath breaking are horrendous. Those who think disciplining Sabbath breakers is harsh must consider for a moment what has happened to our nation. Failing to keep the Sabbath day holy has lead to a departure from God which ultimately leads to our destruction. One example shall be cited which shall suffice. In the ten-year war in Afghanistan, we lost 3,860 men. That would be at a rate of 386 deaths a year. The nation was outraged, calling for our troops to come home. Yet in 2001, there were 667 murders in Chicago—just one city! In 2016, the murder rate increased 72 percent! Yet nothing is said concerning the blood that stains our streets.

How do we explain this horror? How has the Midwestern city of hospitality become a city filled with violence? Have violence and murders in our cities become an acceptable way of life? I pray not! But this is the aftermath of profaning the Sabbath and thus rejecting God. Have we not read in Amos 3:6, "...Shall there be evil in a city, and the LORD hath not done it?" We cannot sin without experiencing Divine retribution!

> Sin against God, a fearful thing!
> O what wrath on us we bring!
> O Let's be true; and let's be wise
> The Sabbath day, do not despise.
> Shall we go on ignoring God?
> Until we drown in our own blood?
> Let us cease to profane His Day?
> And stay this horrid moral decay.

CHAPTER 2

The Law and Love

In reflecting upon the Scriptures and the early Founders of our country, it was understood that to violate the fourth commandment was a very grievous crime. However, some claim that the commandments had been put away when Christ died on our behalf. Because of His atoning work, the commandments are no longer binding, at least, that is, in regard to the believer. Some would have us believe that because we are under grace, we are not to strive to obey the Law. The law through Christ, we are told, has been annulled.

It is quite apparent that our Founding Fathers knew nothing of this teaching! They had a right understanding of sin. So did the primitive church as well. They understood that "...sin is the transgression of the law" (1 John 3:4). If the Law has been put away, as we are being told, then there would be no such thing as sin. After all, the definition of sin is the transgression of the Law. All of which means, no law, no sin! We might as well embrace the amoral if this is our thinking. God forbid such a thought! The church with its antinomian teachings has opened the door for the world to embrace the amoral! Is this not frightening?

It is apparent that the Law still stands, for we are told "For all have sinned, and come short of the glory of God" (Romans 3:23).

It is ONLY through REPENTANCE and FAITH that we find forgiveness! Repentance is understood to be a changing of the mind. In this case, this changing of the mind is a radical change. It is a life of disobedience changed to a life of obedience to the lordship of our Lord Jesus Christ.

Consider how our Founders built the greatest nation in the history of mankind. This is not up for debate. However, they never entertained such foolishness as no law. They understood our Lord when He said,

> Think not that I am come to destroy the law, or the prophets: I am not come to destroy, but to fulfil. For verily I say unto you, Till heaven and earth pass, one jot or one tittle shall in no wise pass from the law, till all be fulfilled (Matthew 5:17-18).

Surely we know that no civilization can exist without law. It is when the Law breaks down that nations fall. Christ did not do away with the Law, but rather He established it.

Furthermore, the apostle Paul tells us that when God converts a soul, He writes His law upon that heart.

> For if that first covenant had been faultless, then should no place have been sought for the second. For finding fault with them, he saith, Behold, the days come, saith the Lord, when I will make a new covenant with the house of Israel and with the house of Judah: Not according to the covenant that I made with their fathers in the day when I took them by the hand to lead them out of the land of Egypt; because they continued not in my covenant, and I regarded them not, saith the Lord. For this is the covenant that I will make with the house of Israel after those days, saith the Lord; I will put my laws into their mind, and write them in their hearts: and I will be to them a God, and they shall be to me a people (Hebrews 8:7-10).

In reading these passages, one should carefully reflect upon the eighth verse. We are told that there was never anything wrong with the Law. The problem was with "them," not with "it." The problem has always been with man. There was never a problem with the Law of God as it is pure, perfect and good. (Read Psalm 119.) In reading the Scriptures, we come to realize the imperativeness of the new birth. Through this Divine operation, God writes His law upon our hearts. We have now become a new creation in Christ Jesus (2 Corinthians 5:17). The change is again stated in Ephesians 1:3-4 wherein we read,

> Blessed be the God and Father of our Lord Jesus Christ,
> who hath blessed us with all spiritual blessings in heavenly
> places in Christ: According as he hath chosen us in
> him before the foundation of the world, that we should
> be holy and without blame before him in love.

And again, we read in 2 Corinthians 10:5,

> Casting down imaginations, and every high thing that
> exalteth itself against the knowledge of God, and bringing
> into captivity every thought to the obedience of Christ.

There is no question of the saints being under grace, but God never did away with the Law. He told us that He did not come to destroy the Law (Matthew 5:17). Neither do those who are born of God find the Law grievous. They find it a delight. And as for the love of God, it is understood in the context of 1 John 5:3. "For this is the love of God, that we keep his commandments: and his commandments are not grievous." If one finds the commandments of God grievous, he would do well to examine himself to see if he is in the faith.

On the contrary, the only things our Lord came to destroy are the devil and the works of the devil. This is what we are told in Hebrews

2:14 and 1 John 3:7. In order to do this, He had to go down into death to destroy the devil who had the power of death (Hebrews 2:14). O the wonder and mystery of the cross!

It is foolish then to speak of the love of God and fail to obey Him. To love the Lord is to obey Him. Yet many are deceived in thinking of love as an emotion. To love as we are commanded is to honor, revere and obey our God. If one does not obey the Lord, then it is apparent that person does not honor Him. How then can that person say that he loves God and at the same time fail to honor Him? Would it not be ludicrous to say "I love the Lord" and at the same time dishonor Him? Yet this is just how deceived men are!

What should ever be kept before us is the Great Commandment. The Lord Himself said that to love the Lord our God with our entire being and to love our neighbor as ourselves were the greatest commandments (Matthew 22:37-38). It is upon these two commandments the entire law and the prophets rest. Thus, the first divine injunction is to love our Lord God with all of our heart, mind, soul and strength. Surely, this would be manifested in a desire to come apart one day in seven to meet with Him. Only the love of the world and the love of the things of the world would expunge the love of God from our hearts. But on the other hand, the love of God in our hearts would expunge the love of the world and the things of the world. These two loves cannot coexist. One or the other must go. If the heart is filled with the love of God, then one would draw nigh unto God; and to such, the Sabbath is a delight.

Where many have gone astray in their thinking is equating love with an emotion. Love is not so much an ardent affection as it is to honor and revere. This does not mean that there are no emotions; however, to love the Lord our God as we are commanded is a Divine imperative upon the will. One cannot command the emotions; it is the will that is enjoined to love God. To love in this context is to honor our Lord above all. We are enjoined to "Owe no man any thing, but to love one another: for he that loveth another hath fulfilled the law" (Romans 13:8). What does this mean? Does it not mean to do good to all men and not sin against them? To sin against a person is to be indebted to that person. Thus we are taught to pray, "And forgive us our debts, as we forgive our debtors" (Matthew 6:12).

The Greek word that is translated "love" in the above passages is αγαπε, (agape). Αγαπε (agape) means "to hold in the highest esteem." This love is manifested in a life of obedience. On the other hand, Πιλω (philo), which is another Greek word for love, refers to the affections. The word "love" enjoining us to love our Lord with our entire being is αγαπε (agape) which means to honor, esteem and obey. Our Lord does not command the affections but the will. We are commanded to honor our Lord in the highest and to do so is manifested in a life of obedience.

Trench, in his work, *Synonyms of the New Testament*, addresses the difference between the two words "philo" and "agape." He gives an example from Mark Antony's address to the people in eulogizing Caesar. He said, "I loved (philo) him as a father and esteemed or honored (Agape) him as a benefactor." [4] (εφιλησατε αυτον ως πατερα, κια ηγαπησατε ως ευεργετην.)

Now we can understand why the man was stoned for gathering sticks on the Sabbath. He was dishonoring God. He did not love Him but rather dishonored Him. It is written, "For them that honour me I will honour, and they that despise me shall be lightly esteemed" (1 Samuel 2:30). If we love the Lord, we will obey Him. And if we obey Him, then we will surely "Remember the Sabbath day, to keep it holy."

---

[4] Archbishop Richard Chenevix Trench D.D., *Synonyms of the New Testament* (Grand Rapids, MI: Associated Publishers and Authors Inc.), 38.

Away with this foolishness that the Law has passed away or that it is not binding upon the believer. Those who are of this mind would do well to meditate upon the 119th Psalm. Following are just a few verses from Psalm 119, revealing the heart of a true child of God. For example, verse 70 "…but I delight in thy law," verse 77 "…thy law is my delight," and verse 97 "O how love I thy law! it is my meditation all the day." All of these are the expressions of the true child of God's heart. Away with the thought that the Law passed away or that the Law is oppressive. The law is the rule of God which is full of grace.

> Men glibly say, "Lord I love Thee,
> You are everything to me".
> However they do not obey;
> Failing to keep the Sabbath day.
>
> He said if thou wilt honor Me
> Then I too shall honor thee.
> But if thou wilt despise me,
> Then I too, shall despise thee.
>
> Hence to love is to obey
> It is to walk in the narrow way.
> If we love God with all our might,
> We'll call the Sabbath a delight?

CHAPTER 3

Which Is the Most Essential Commandment?

If one should inquire which commandment is the Great Commandment, the only answer one could honestly give is the one that our Lord gave when the question was put to Him by a certain scribe. He answered:

> And thou shalt love the Lord thy God with all thy heart, and with
> all thy soul, and with all thy mind, and with all thy strength:
> this is the first commandment. And the second is like, namely
> this, Thou shalt love thy neighbour as thyself. There is none
> other commandment greater than these (Mark 12:30-31).

To love God with our entire being and to love our neighbor as ourselves no doubt are the greatest commandments. In doing this, one fulfills the entire law in his relationship to God as well as to man. As for this scribe, he confessed that our Lord had answered well, and, in turn, our Lord said that he was not far from the Kingdom of God.

Therefore, in reflecting upon the Ten Commandments, we should realize that they all stand or fall together. To offend in one does not give us a passing grade of 90 percent but rather a zero. To fail in one command means that we are guilty of a capital crime, and the sentence is death. James tells us, "For whosoever shall keep the whole law, and yet offend in one point, he is guilty of all" (James 2:10). Therefore, one should consider the Ten Commandments as a whole since they are "the Law" and not "the laws."

This idea is sobering as we have a tendency to view some commandments as less important than others. As for the fourth commandment, presently it is not taken seriously. However, to violate any one of the Ten Commandments demands the offender's damnation. As for the apostle Paul, he had come to realize this when he confessed, "…I had not known sin, but by the law: for I had not known lust, except the law had said, Thou shalt not covet" (Romans 7:7). It was then he discovered that he was a transgressor **of the Law.** We know that when he referred to the Law he was actually referring to the tenth commandment. He knew to offend in one point was to offend in all. Hence, it stands to reason that if one violates the fourth commandment, he or she is an offender of the Law as the commandments stand together as one.

Yet at the same time, they are ten individual commandments, the fact of which is undeniable. Therefore, one may rightly inquire which commandment of the ten is the most crucial. After much thought, we would be forced to conclude that it is the fourth commandment. This commandment is the most critical of them all. This may sound strange to the reader because, as mentioned earlier, many do not consider Sabbath observance to be moral. It is viewed more or less as a ritual. But nothing is further from the truth. It would be helpful to briefly reflect upon the first four commandments as these are the weightiest.

The first commandment tells us whom we are to worship. We are commanded, "Thou shalt have no other gods before me" (Exodus 20:3). We are to worship Jehovah, our God, and Him only. We are to have no other god but Jehovah. Jehovah alone is to be revered and served. He will have no rivals.

Consider when Satan tempted our Lord in the wilderness, offering Him all the kingdoms of the world if our Lord would only worship him. Our Lord replied, "…Get thee hence, Satan: for it is written, Thou shalt worship the Lord thy God, and him only shalt thou serve" (Matthew 4:10). Our Lord repelled Satan's attack, reminding him of the first commandment.

Also, we should observe that worship and service go together. We serve that which we worship. Interesting that Satan said nothing about service. However, we know that our God is a jealous God, and He alone is to be worshiped which also includes service. How many are conscious of being idolaters who serve themselves yet with their lips profess to worship God?

The second commandment tells us the manner in which we are to worship. **Worship is spiritual.** We are not to make any graven images, yet men to this day make their images of God in spite of this Divine injunction. These images are not only statues and paintings but also images which we have created in our minds of what we think God is like. There are some who, if corrected with the Scriptures, will become angry and say, "Well, your God is not my God." What they say is true. They have a god of their own making which is not the God of the Bible. We must be careful not to create a god of our own making. This is the highest form of idolatry.

Neither should it be surprising that men create so many images of God. When corrected, they tell us that these images help them to worship. However, the only ones who can actually worship God are those born from above. One must be born again. Worship is spiritual.

The new birth is a divine imperative. This truth becomes pronounced in John 4:24. Our Lord, in addressing the woman at the well, said, "God is a Spirit: and they that worship him must worship him in spirit and in truth." This divine imperative is what is stressed in this second commandment. It should not be surprising that lost humanity, being spiritually dead, depends upon various images to help in worship. But our God forbids it, all of which should drive men to seek Him with all of their hearts.

Then the third commandment tells us how we are to worship. God is to be revered. We are not to come before Him casually or irreverently. Neither are we to take His name lightly on our lips. To do so is blasphemous. God is to be feared above all. We are to approach Him in godly reverence. This does not mean we do not rejoice in His presence, but it does mean we are not to come flippantly before Him. The contemporary worship of our day is blasphemous. It is a gross violation of the third commandment.

What does this have to say of contemporary music? How many are guilty of a capital crime and are not aware of it! There are more blasphemers in the churches than of common men on the streets. When we come before the Lord we are to come with godly reverence. He is to be honored above all. These contemporary worship services are a gross violation of the third commandment.

When we come to the fourth commandment, we are told when we are to cease from all labors and come apart to worship God. If we do not come apart one in seven days to worship our Lord, then we will forget all of the other commandments. This is what makes the fourth commandment so critical. If we fail to observe the Sabbath, we will not only forget all of the other commandments, but we shall also forget God. As one can readily see, the fourth commandment stands in some respect as the most crucial of them all as it serves as the bulwark for all of the others.

When reading the New Testament, it is apparent that the Jews were profoundly conscious of the mandate to observe the Sabbath. This is especially true in reading the gospels. Reflecting upon the early part of our Lord's ministry, the religious leaders, as well as the people, received our Lord with gladness. They were drawn to Him and in earnest attended to His teaching.

An example of this is found in the fifth chapter of Luke. Our Lord was teaching in a certain house and the religious leaders came from afar to hear Him expound the things of God. There were so many people present that the house was packed, so much so that no one could enter through the door. Therefore, four men bearing a friend on a stretcher had to open up the roof and lower their friend down into the house in order to bring him to our Lord. Then our Lord said something startling. He forgave the man of his sin.

With that, the religious leaders began to murmur among themselves. They reasoned in their hearts, "Why doth this man thus speak blasphemies? who can forgive sins but God only" (Mark 2:7). Knowing their thoughts, our Lord demonstrated He had the power to forgive sin by commanding the man to rise and take his bed and walk. Then we read when that happened, they all marveled. They were all astonished. At this time, there was no open hostility toward our Lord.

However, conflict began when our Lord healed a man on the Sabbath day. In the fifth chapter of John, we have the record of our Lord healing the lame man who helplessly lay by the pool of Bethesda. The Lord not only healed him but commanded him to take up his bed and walk. He was not to leave his bed behind. He was to take it with him. Immediately, the man responded by doing as he was commanded. He took up his bed and walked.

When the Jews saw this man walking and carrying his bed on the Sabbath, they were alarmed. Immediately, they corrected the man saying what he was doing was not lawful. He then informed them that He Who made him whole commanded him to take up his bed and walk. In outrage they demanded, "Tell us who this man is!" When they discovered that it was Jesus, they were determined to put Him to death. It is interesting that the Jews never forgave our Lord of this one good work (See John 7:21). This was because, as they saw it, He was a Sabbath breaker.

This Sabbath conflict was what eventually led to His crucifixion. To them it was apparent, as they saw it, that our Lord violated the fourth commandment. This was a capital crime which demanded His death. He not only violated the fourth commandment, but it also appeared that He encouraged others to do the same. Therefore, they moved to remedy the situation before it got out of hand. They would not for a moment tolerate the desecration of the Sabbath.

Today, some present the Pharisees to us as blind, envious bigots. They are seen as extremists in determining to put all Sabbath breakers to death. But does not the Law require this? They understood the seriousness of this crime. They may not have understood the intent of the Law, but they understood that Sabbath breakers were to be put to death. We know that our Lord never violated the fourth commandment as some suggest. However, these Jews understood that which this contemporary generation of Christians fails to understand. They knew that if Sabbath breakers were not executed, then they, as a peculiar people of God, would soon lose their distinction. In time, the nation would fall away to the world, and the people would become apostates. They would become even as the Gentiles whom they abhorred. (Does not history bear record to this?) Therefore, they were right in jealously guarding the Sabbath. But they were wrong in understanding how the Sabbath was to be observed.

Today, the transgression of the fourth commandment does not appear to be a great crime. Many churches increasingly are having Saturday night services so that people can recreate on the Lord's Day. Others, as soon as the morning service is over, go out and dine or even go shopping. Others work on the Sabbath as if it were just another day. As most professing Christians see it, they have fulfilled their religious duty if they attend the morning service. They are of the mind that God would not be angry with them if they work, play and recreate on the Sabbath. Is it any wonder that the nation has become godless and violence is in our streets?

Those Jews who are often criticized had a better understanding of Sabbath observance than most professing Christians. They understood that the observance of the Sabbath insured the preservation of their faith and the perpetuity of their nation. They understood that if they failed to keep the Sabbath day holy, they would become apostates. This ultimately did lead to their destruction. Regardless of what we may say of these religious Pharisees, they understood something our generation fails to understand. They understood, "The wicked shall be turned into hell, and all the nations that forget God" (Psalm 9:17).

They also knew that there were no exceptions. Those religious leaders were profoundly conscious of the reason why their nation was destroyed and why the people had gone into captivity. The nation had profaned the Sabbath and, in time, had become as apostate as the other nations around them. In failing to observe the Sabbath, they had become idolaters. The unacceptable had become acceptable as the people openly practiced harlotry and homosexuality. As for the temple of God, it became polluted, and, in time, God departed.

Jeremiah prophesied up until the fall of the nation calling the people to repentance. It is interesting what he admonished the nation to do. In Jeremiah 17:27 we read,

But if ye will not hearken unto me to hallow the sabbath day, and not to bear a burden, even entering in at the gates of Jerusalem on the sabbath day; then will I kindle a fire in the gates thereof, and it shall devour the palaces of Jerusalem, and it shall not be quenched.

As we are aware, the people would not hear. They had forgotten God, and heathen temples and abominable practices filled the land. Hence, the LORD spewed them out of the land as those who were there before them. Then the land enjoyed seventy years of Sabbaths as it lay desolate.

In light of the seriousness of failing to observe the fourth commandment, consider where we, as a nation, have fallen. We too have forgotten our God. For decades, churches have been closing, and heathen temples and mosques are popping up everywhere. Not only has violence become pronounced, but the saints who seek to honor the Lord are persecuted. They are hated because they do not accept homosexuality, abortions, and the transgender movement, to mention a few. The unthinkable has become the norm. All restraints are being lifted under the guise of "human rights." Not to comply with the movement is to be looked upon as a bigot and one who hates people.

The nation has forgotten how to blush. What happened? Where have we gone astray? We failed to heed the exhortation, "Remember the Sabbath day, to keep it holy." In failing to observe the Sabbath as we are commanded, we have forgotten all of the other commandments. We have also forgotten that it was God Who had made us great. The perpetuity of the faith and the continuance of the nation presently lie in the balances.

It is astounding that there is a call to Christians to repentance. But they are not told from what they must repent. However, they are exhorted to fast and pray. 2 Chronicles 7:14 preaches,

> If my people, which are called by my name, shall humble
> themselves, and pray, and seek my face, and turn from
> their wicked ways; then will I hear from heaven, and
> will forgive their sin, and will heal their land.

But this text is left without meaning. Many fast and pray but are not heard! Why such silence from God? What is the problem?

Consider what our Lord had to say to Israel through His prophet Jeremiah before the nation fell. Those times in which he prophesied were times such as these! We know Jeremiah did not merely quote 2 Chronicles 7:14. Neither did he merely exhort the people to fast and pray. He exhorted the people to action saying,

> And it shall come to pass, if ye diligently hearken unto me,
> saith the Lord, to bring in no burden through the gates of
> this city on the sabbath day, but hallow the sabbath day,
> to do no work therein; Then shall there enter into the gates
> of this city kings and princes sitting upon the throne of
> David, riding in chariots and on horses, they, and their
> princes, the men of Judah, and the inhabitants of Jerusalem:
> and this city shall remain for ever (Jeremiah 17:24-25).

He called them to observe the Sabbath and to keep it holy. But as we know, they did not heed the call. There were people who fasted and prayed even as we have people doing today. However, such prayers are vain if they are not accompanied with repentance and obedience.

Today, we do not hear the admonition to hallow the Sabbath coming from our pulpits. Why is this? Can it be that we have failed to realize how crucial the fourth commandment is? Have we failed to realize that it serves as a bulwark for all the other commandments? But, alas, we have become a nation that has no fear of God before our eyes! We have become even as Friedrich Nietzsche had prophesied through his prophet Zarathustra, "…There is no devil, and no hell. Thy soul will be dead even sooner than thy body: fear therefore nothing." [5]

When we depart from our Lord, our soul dies and our bodies soon follow. Is it any wonder that suicide is becoming the leading cause of death? Christ Jesus is our Life! We must draw nigh to Him! We must hallow the Sabbath day. It is a must!

> Can one not know that He is dead
> As he lies upon his bed?
> And let the Sabbath day go by
> And unto God does not draw nigh?
>
> It's the soul within that dies
> Before in death we close our eyes.
> And then what shall become of thee?
> When God's frown that day you see!
>
> Honor thou the Sabbath day
> T'was made for thee to come away.
> And find the Christ Who died for thee
> That from sin thou be free.

---

[5] Friedrich Nietzsche, *Search for the meaning of life* (NY, Chicago, San Francisco: Holt, Rinehart & Winston, 1962), 362.

CHAPTER 4

When Was the Sabbath Instituted?

When addressing the subject of the Sabbath, many are inclined to think that the Sabbath is merely a Hebrew institution. They equate it with the Hebrew people and with the time of their coming out of Egypt. No doubt when the Hebrew people came out of Egypt, they had to be instructed in the Law of God. After all, they were enslaved for over four hundred years, and during that period, they had forgotten many things in regard to the ways of the Lord. If one has a difficulty in understanding why, then let us look at ourselves and consider how far we have fallen way from the Lord and in much less time--and we are not slaves.

But God had not forgotten them, and in time, He brought them out of their bondage with a great and mighty arm. After being delivered from under the tyrannical rule of Pharaoh, the Hebrew people were led to Sinai. Jehovah, through Moses, instructed the nation in the ways in which they were to live. They had to be taught the Law of the LORD. But this time, instead of passing on His law by word of mouth, our Lord wrote the commandments upon tables of stone. It is especially interesting that the fourth commandment commences with the word "remember." None of the other commandments begin that way. This in itself is striking. Should we not inquire, "Why does this fourth commandment commence with the exhortation to 'remember'?"

It is apparent that this was not the first time the command of Sabbath observance was enjoined to man. One does not exhort another to remember something that was not formerly known although it may be said that the word "remember" is a divine mandate implying "do not forget." We indeed must understand this to be true. We use the word "remember" in this same way when instructing our children. After giving instructions, we admonish them to remember what we have said, and we may even repeat what we said in order to make a lasting impression upon their minds. No doubt our Lord also used the word "remember" in this way.

But there is more to understand by this exhortation since our Lord did not enjoin the people to remember any of the other nine commandments. After all, are we not to remember to keep all of the other nine commandments as well? Of course we are. It is apparent, then, by the wording of the fourth commandment that to "remember" is not restrictively meant "not to forget." The word "remember" addresses the memory to recall that which was formerly known. Hence, this Divine mandate seeks to awaken the memory.

It is apparent that God had ordained from the creation of the world that man should observe the Sabbath day and keep it holy. Nevertheless, there are some who are of the opinion that the Law given at Sinai was only for the Hebrew nation. No doubt at this time, their government was being established, and laws were being instituted. Moses was their great lawgiver. This is not up for debate.

Then others assume the call to remember is to be understood in the context of the people going out to gather manna on the Sabbath. We recall there were those who went out on the Sabbath to gather manna and came up short because they did not heed the command of Moses. Therefore, it is said by some that the "Sabbath" was first mentioned in Exodus 16:23. Thus, the antecedent of this exhortation to remember goes back no further than when the Hebrew people were instructed in the gathering of manna.

No doubt there is an element of truth in that which is said. On that first Sabbath after the manna was given, some indeed went out to gather manna and found none. This is seen in Exodus chapter sixteen. However, in reading the fourth commandment in its entirety, the memory of the hearers is taken back to Genesis. For in the 11th verse, it is said, "For in six days the Lord made heaven and earth, the sea, and all that in them is, and rested the seventh day: wherefore the Lord blessed the sabbath day, and hallowed it."

Hence, our Lord had taken Moses and the people back to Genesis 2:2-3. There it is stated that God, after creating all things, rested on the seventh day. The nation was now exhorted to follow His example. This Divine precept was established from the creation of the world. It is imperative that this is understood.

In Genesis 2:2-3, we have the first mentioning of the Sabbath. God, at this time, holds Himself before men as their example that we should do even as He did. As for the word "rested" in Genesis 2:2, it is the Hebrew word "Shebeth" which is understood to be a "Sabbath rest." It is a ceasing from labor. Thus, when we are exhorted to "remember," we are to reflect upon the beginning of time, when God had instituted the Sabbath. It was on the seventh day of creation that God instituted the Sabbath. It was not only observed by God Who rested from all His works, but it was also observed by Adam as well.

The Sabbath was instituted before the fall of man. It was instituted before sin had ever entered into the world. Moreover, it was instituted long before there ever was a nation called Israel. It was instituted centuries before Abraham was ever born. The fourth commandment should never be thought of as something that is particular to the Hebrew people. Neither should it be thought to be an ordinance limited to the Old Covenant. What we should realize is that the command to "remember the Sabbath day" resurfaces at this time when the nation of Israel was being established. It is without question that the Sabbath had its beginning from the creation of the world.

Therefore, the Divine mandate to observe the Sabbath is a universal injunction. It is a mandate that includes all mankind, as all humanity is out of the loins of Adam. Everyone, regardless of nation, race, color, or location, is commanded to "Remember the Sabbath day, to keep it holy." Is it any wonder that this mandate commences with the word "REMEMBER"?

It is clearly understood in the wording of the fourth commandment who should observe the Sabbath. We must not overlook that servants, animals, and strangers who were also enjoined to a Hebrew family were required to observe this Divine mandate. The strangers were Gentiles. Thus, the Gentiles, as well as the Hebrew people, were to observe the Sabbath. Just simply meditating on the fourth commandment and looking no further, it is evident that this divine mandate, as all the others, is universally binding.

Therefore, in addressing the doctrine of the Sabbath, one is compelled to go back to Genesis. The hermeneutical principle, "the law of first mention," demands this. One cannot rightly address the doctrine of the Sabbath without going back to where it was first mentioned. This is because where the doctrine is first mentioned never loses its meaning. The doctrine may grow in understanding but it never changes its meaning—never!

What is of further interest is that Adam was created on the sixth day. This means that Adam's first full day was a Sabbath. His first full day was a day filled with wonder and worship. It is hard for us to imagine, when his eyes were first opened to behold everything, the impression that God's creation must have made upon His soul. In his pristine state, he saw, he knew, he understood, and he worshipped his Creator! He was not created to be an infant but rather a full-grown man having perfect understanding. Therefore, he began with a full day of worship, and on the following day, he was fitted for work. He tilled the garden and named the animals, having dominion over all creation and serving as vice regent under his Creator.

Since God instituted the Sabbath on the seventh day, He also ordained two other things that are inescapable. The first is that God created the world in six literal days. These days were from evening until morning. These days are not figurative but actually six days that run from evening to morning as the earth spins on its axis. There was no evolutionary process by which our God made the heavens and the earth.

Secondly, God had a purpose in creating the world in six days. We know He could have created all things in the twinkling of an eye, but He did not choose to do so. We know that He will do just that when He returns to make all things new. He will create a new Heaven and earth at the time of His appearing. The first creation could well have been accomplished just as quickly as the new creation which will take place when time is swallowed up in eternity. But He did not choose to do that, and it was for a good reason. God had a definite purpose in creating the world in six days. It was in order to establish a seven-day week. On the seventh day, we are to cease from all labor and follow His example in observing the Sabbath.

One should also observe that when the Sabbath was instituted, man had not as yet sinned. Man was in his pristine state. The curse had not yet fallen upon the earth. In fact, when God looked upon all that He had created, He said it was very good (Genesis 1:31). This includes the Sabbath which was instituted immediately following the

Creation. All of this shows that man, even in his pristine state, needs a Sabbath. How much more do we need to observe the Sabbath in our fallen state!

What should be impressed upon our minds is that the observance of the Sabbath is universal. It has nothing to do with whether a person is a Jew or Gentile. God instituted the Sabbath from the beginning of the world which, in itself, is telling because it reveals to us without any equivocation that "man," regardless of where he is found on earth, is to come apart one day in seven and worship his Creator. God had thus ordained this from the beginning of time.

Before leaving this matter, we should observe that there were also two other things that God instituted in Paradise. These also are universal. The first thing that God instituted was work. He placed man in the garden to keep it. Work is not the result of sin. Work is a ministry; it is the blessing of serving. Man was made to serve. He was never made to be useless doing nothing; neither was he made to serve himself. God meant for him to be productive. It was only after the fall that man was to eat his bread by the sweat of his brow. But regardless after the fall or before the fall, man universally was ordained to work. In 2 Thessalonians 3:10, the apostle writes, "…if any would not work, neither should he eat." Does this not take us back to Genesis?

This was understood by all the Hebrew people since everyone was to learn a trade. Rabbis and Pharisees were required to have a trade of some sort. They were either cobblers, carpenters, or tentmakers (as was the apostle Paul) and so forth. They would work with their hands even though they had degrees equivalent to those in our day who hold doctorates. They would not think for a moment of not working and thus being denied the privilege to minister to their fellow man. They understood that God from the creation had made us to be productive.

The second thing God instituted in paradise was marriage. Marriage of one man to one woman is God's law that applies to man universally. Our Lord in addressing the subject of marriage takes the reader back to Genesis (Matthew 19:4-6). Marriage also was instituted before the fall. Hence in paradise, God instituted worship, work, and marriage, and marriage was with the intent to reproduce and populate the world. All three of these are universally binding upon all humanity. It is precisely in that order that God ordained them. God created man, whether Jew or Gentile, to worship his Maker, to work with his hands, and to marry and replenish the earth. If marriage and work are universal, then why would one ever think that the Sabbath observance is not universally binding as well? It should never be thought that the mandate of Sabbath observance had ceased or that it is only binding for the Hebrew people.

If the observance of the Sabbath ceased as many claim, what shall we say of marriage and work? Have these also ceased? If so, then one might have an argument for the Sabbath observance to cease. But as long as there is time, these three things will never cease. In eternity these three will also continue. The bride will be united to the Bridegroom from Whose pierced side she was formed. She will be His helpmeet who will reign with Him throughout eternity with joy. And she also shall rejoice in that one eternal Sabbath as time will be no more.

O Blessed Holy Sabbath Morn
From Creation Thou wast born
A token of Eternal rest
For the saints forever blessed.

Oh the trials of the week
Leaves our souls both tried and weak!
How we groan for that blessed day
When Thou shall wipe all tears away!

But this Day that's above all days
Sustains that which our soul doth crave.
From all labors we're set free
To come and spend the day with Thee.

CHAPTER 5

The Sabbath Was Made for Man

Our Lord, in addressing the Jews, said, "The Sabbath was made for man." Again, one should realize by this declaration that the Sabbath was not merely a Jewish institution. This truth cannot be overstressed in this day of confusion. It has been shown from Scripture that the fourth commandment is universally binding upon all humanity. Therefore, we must never entertain the thought of the Sabbath as a Hebrew institution. From the creation of the world, all humanity is enjoined to keep the Sabbath day holy. One may inquire that if the Sabbath were made for man, surely there should be historical records where men other than the Jews observed the Sabbath. What may surprise many is that at one time, all humanity universally observed the Sabbath, also being conscious of all the other commandments that are set forth in the Decalogue.

The commandments are most pronounced in regard to the Hebrew people because God called them out from among the nations unto Himself that through them He would preserve the truth and bring forth the Redeemer. We must keep in mind that God committed the "Holy Oracles" to the Jews (Romans 3:2). We see further that God chose the Hebrew people to maintain a witness in the world. They were to be evangelists. They were never meant to be exclusively separated from humanity. They were meant to enlighten

31

all humanity which was engulfed in darkness. This does not imply that they were not to be a holy, separated people. However, no one can read the 100th Psalm and fail to see that their mission was to be God's witnesses in the world. This Psalm is but one of many examples of God's intent in separating Abraham and raising up a holy nation unto Himself. All the nations were to be blessed through his "Seed" which is Christ (Galatians 3:16).

But aside from all this, let us consider how all humanity at one time observed the Sabbath. In the Antediluvian period, our Lord maintained a witness of Himself to men. Some may argue that there is no record of Sabbath observances during this period of man's history, but this is not true. This period covered some 1,678 years. It spanned a length of time from the creation of the world to the Great Deluge. All that took place during this period is not recorded. However, the word "seventh" as well as "seven" is repeatedly mentioned in ancient writings, indicating that people had observed a seven-day week which concluded with a Sabbath observance.

For example, in Genesis 7:1-4, we read that God told Noah to enter the Ark **seven days** before the rains and floods came. Genesis 7:10 also states that it was on the **seventh day** after Noah and his house entered into the Ark that the rains and floods came upon the earth. The seventh day is always in reference to the Sabbath. Thus, it was on the Sabbath, when men refused to repent, that the flood waters came upon the earth. In the ark, Noah and his house found rest from the wrath of God on the Sabbath day. What a picture of Sabbatical rest!

After the waters subsided, Noah sent a dove which returned to the ark as it found no rest. Genesis 8:10 says that before he sent the dove a second time, **he waited seven days, or one week,** after the waters subsided. Then Noah waited another seven days, or another week, before he again sent the dove (Genesis 8:12). This number "seven" is frequently mentioned which is no mere coincidence. It is quite apparent that the seventh day has reference to the Sabbath as well as to the seven-day week. The Sabbath was observed by the godly during this period of man's history.

Now all that has been said thus far may seem subjective. But when we consider the history of mankind after the flood as the world began to repopulate, we discover that men observed the Sabbath. How do we explain this if Sabbath worship were not handed down to humanity through the eight who survived the Great Deluge? One may inquire, "Do we actually know that men observed the Sabbath, or is this a mere assumption?"

To the surprise of many, we have historical records that bear witness of men after the flood hallowing the seventh day. Those nations in the Fertile Crescent, from which the earth was repopulated, were faithful to keep the Sabbath day holy. All of this reveals that the Sabbath was indeed made for man. It also reveals that those who survived the Flood not only observed the Sabbath but also taught the coming generation to do the same. We possess early historical records of those nations in the Fertile Crescent that reveal how they indeed hallowed the Seventh Day. Thus man, before becoming an apostate, hallowed the Sabbath day.

One would find it very interesting to read Smith's famous work, *Assyrian Research*. Smith states that the Assyrians, at one time, faithfully kept the Sabbath day holy. On this subject, Smith writes,

> In the year 1869, I discovered among other things a curious religious calendar of the Assyrians in which every month is divided into four weeks and the seventh day or 'Sabbath' are marked out as days in which no work should be undertaken.[6]

---

[6] George Smith, *Assyrian Discoveries* (New York: Scribner, Armstrong & Co., 1875), 12.

Who would have ever thought that the Assyrians, during the time of Abraham, would have been observers of the Sabbath? All we know of them, or all that we are taught of them, is that they were a wicked, brutal, and ruthless people who crushed nations. But little do we know of their fear of God. It is apparent that they had some truth, for many years later when Jonah came preaching, they repented, humbling themselves in sackcloth and ashes. It is believed that Jonah was buried in Assyria. However, it is obvious that the Assyrians had some knowledge of God. This knowledge was not only retained in Israel but also in the nations of the Gentiles.

Then there are the discoveries of Sayce. He too sheds great light on this subject. In his studies of ancient archives, he addresses the word "Sabbath" and how it was used by several ancient countries that dwelt in the Fertile Crescent. He writes,

> The study of foreign tongues naturally brought with it an inquisitiveness about the language of other people as well as a passion for etymology. The latter led grammarians to invent Accadian etymologies for the Teutonic words in English by dictionary-makers of a former generation. Thus we find Sabattu of Sabatuv 'The Sabbath' derived from two Accadian words sa 'the heart' and bat 'to end' and accordingly explained to mean 'a day of rest for the heart'. The inquisitiveness about foreign languages produced a better result. We owe to it preservation of the meaning of several words in ancient languages of Elam, and of other countries by which Babylonia was surrounded.[7]

Sayce again observes rules of Sabbath observances by the Assyrians and the Babylonians, both great empires before Israel became a nation. He writes,

---

[7] A. H. Sayce, *Social Life Among the Assyrians and the Babylonians* (New York: Fleming H. Revel Co., 1893), Vol. xviii, 38.

The Babylonians and the Assyrians, kept a Sabbattu or Sabbath
which a Babylonian writer described as 'a day of rest for the
heart.' It was observed on the 7th, 14th, 19th, 21st, and 28th,
of each day of the month and on it all kinds of work were
disallowed. No food was to be cooked, no new garments
put on, no medicine taken. The king was forbidden to ride
his chariot and even the prophets forbidden to prophesy.[8]

Both of these empires of the Fertile Crescent were strict observers
of the Sabbath. It is interesting to note that they had prophets. This
explains the prophet Balaam, does it not?

From the preponderance of evidences, it is apparent that the
Gentiles observed the Sabbath before there was a Hebrew nation.
It is also evident that the law of Sabbath observance was given to
all humanity. It is universal as the fourth commandment is binding
upon all men. Furthermore, one cannot help but notice that the
Babylonian Sabbaths came every seven days with an extra one added
in the month. This is arresting since the Babylonians are known to
us as hardened heathens with no fear of God, yet they too kept the
Sabbath day holy. How did this come about if it were not handed
down to them through those eight souls who repopulated the earth
after the Great Deluge!

We also have other witnesses who point to nations observing the
Sabbath. We have the testimony of Theophilus, bishop of Caesarea,
in A. D. 190. In writing to Autolycus, he states,

> Moreover they spake concerning the seventh day which
> all men acknowledge, but most know not that what

---

[8] (Sayce, *Social Life Among the Assyrians and the Babylonians*, Vol. xviii, 121)

among the Hebrews is called the "seventh" (εβδομος)
a name which is adopted by every nation.[9]

The argument of Theophilus is a very strong witness that every nation observed a seven-day week and called the seventh day a Sabbath. However, in time, they fell away. They no doubt observed the Sabbath for a time until they became apostates. However, even after they fell away, they still continued to observe a seven-day week which was established from the creation of the world.

This, by the way, is true worldwide to this day. Every nation still observes the seven-day week, even those who are atheistic. Every nation acknowledges the Sabbath, but their people no longer reverence it. Yet there remain remnants, even to this day, who faithfully observe the Sabbath even though the world, for the most part, has departed from God.

Also, we must not overlook the witness of Josephus. In his writings against Apion, he points out how the Gentiles observed the Sabbath. He writes, "That there could be found no city, either of the Grecians or Barbarians who owned not a seventh day rest from labor." [10] As for Apion, he did not refute what was said because what was said was indisputable.

However, that which is arresting in Josephus' testimony is that the cultivated and barbarians alike observed the Sabbath. It was universally observed by all men, civilized and uncivilized, Greek as well as barbarian. Josephus, a Hebrew priest and general fighting against Rome who lived during and after the fall of Jerusalem, conclusively reveals that the Sabbath was universally acknowledged

---

[9] Theophilus "To Autolycus", *Ante-Nicene Fathers* (New York: Charles Scribner's Son, 1913), Vol. 2, 99.

[10] F. Josephus, *The Complete Works of Josephus* (Grand Rapids, MI: Kregel Pub., 1981), 636.

even in his days. In this testimony, Josephus affirms that a Sabbath observance was not merely Hebrew.

In light of the preponderance of such evidence, how can anyone affirm that the Sabbath was only binding upon the Jews and then, in time, was rescinded? It is imperative that we keep in mind that our Lord said, "…The Sabbath was made for man…" (Mark 2:27). By this declaration alone, our Lord made it clear that the Sabbath is to be observed by all humanity. This is not mere conjecture on my part. It is indisputable that all humanity, at one time, understood that our Lord had ordained the Sabbath for man, not only for the Hebrews but also for every person.

For those who reject or even question what has been stated thus far, there are a few questions to consider. First, how did man ever come to calculate time? Well, one may say that is simple. The measurement of the day is how long it takes the earth to make one complete revolution on its axis. Thus, from evening to morning, we have the measurement of a day. It is as the Lord said; a day is from evening to morning. From this calculation, we are able to further calculate hours, minutes, and seconds.

But how have we come up with the measurement of months? It is interesting that both the Gregorian and Julian calendars have a twelve-month year. Man calculated months by the phases of the moon or how long it takes the moon to make one revolution around the earth. Hence, the celestial clock not only gives us seconds, minutes, hours, and days but also gives us our months.

Now we consider how we are able to calculate 365 days in a year. Did we just pull that number out of the sky? No! Man calculated a year by counting the days it takes the earth to make its journey around the sun, which is 365 days. So now man is able to calculate the length of a year. Thus, we are able to calculate time by seconds, minutes, hours, days, months, years, decades, centuries, and so on. We have a precise universal clock by which we set our watches.

But now the question with which we are faced is how did we ever come up with a seven-day week? A seven-day week is universally observed, yet we have no natural explanation for this because there is no way to account for a seven-day week by our universal clock. Universally, however, all nations have observed a seven-day week. Man observed a seven-day week before and after the Flood. Surely, this should be of interest to any thinking soul. If it were left to man, he would have probably settled for a ten-day week. But no, we have a seven-day week. Is this not arresting? This is the question we all must honestly face. How did this come about and when did this actually come into practice?

The only answer is that God, from the creation of the world, ordained a seven-day week. He worked six days to create the heavens and the earth and on the seventh day, He rested from all of His labors (Genesis 2:2 and Hebrews 4:4). Hence, the seven-day week finds its origin in the creation wherein God had ordained the Sabbath day. There is no other explanation for it. Furthermore, all humanity from Adam to this day observes a seven-day week.

Other fragments of a universal observance of the Sabbath are apparent in how many nations around the world refer to the seventh day as the Sabbath. For example, the Spanish-speaking world refers to the seventh day as "Sabado" which means "Sabbath" in English. This is the same with the Portuguese which is also "Sabado."

The Italians refer to the seventh day as "Sabato." The Greek word for the seventh day is Σάββατο (Sabbato). In Ukranian, it is субота which is the same in Russian, essentially meaning "Sabbath." These are but a few examples that remain unto this day, revealing how man universally understood that the seventh day of the week was the Sabbath.

Of further interest is how men during the French Revolution wanted to do away with God. They substituted the Trinity of Father, Son, and Holy Ghost for Fraternity, Liberty, and Equality. Then to escape from God, they did away with the seven-day week and established a ten-day week. They named their months after seasons of the year. They even began to count time from when the revolution had taken power. Year One was September 1793.

The revolution became so horrifying that one of its leaders said that France had become one gigantic grave yard. Another leader of France said that France had become a gigantic Golgotha. They guillotined people on the flimsiest of grounds. It became so horrible that the people began to fear for their own lives, not trusting anyone, not even their neighbors. Robespierre, a formidable leader of the revolution who guillotined many, was himself guillotined. Even Dr. Guillotine who invented the guillotine was guillotined. France was one horrifying hell on earth as people were out of control.

The people were so out of control because every man was free to do as he pleased, which is the essence of "human rights." Life in France became so terrible that the people overwhelmingly made Napoleon Emperor for life to escape from liberty without God. Thus in 1805, after 12 years of nightmare, they returned to a seven-day week and dated the year 1805 in the year of our Lord. No nation can survive without God! History bears witness to this. And no nation can survive when it ignores a Sabbath observance because, in time, the people of that nation will forget God.

If one questions the necessity of a Sabbath observance, consider how nations throughout the world have fallen into decay. America has fallen into horrible decay by ignoring the Sabbath. At one time, we could live with unlocked doors and windows. We were not afraid to entertain strangers. Whoever knocked on the door was welcomed. As for hitchhikers, we would stop and pick them up and give them a ride. But all of this has changed. Now we live in self-imprisoned homes with barred windows and doors or in gated communities, a euphemism for self-imprisonment facilities. Life has become short, nasty, and brutish.

As for our schools, the plea at one time was for more teachers and smaller classrooms. Now, however, the plea is for more policemen to protect children from killing one another or their teachers. And as for our policemen, they were "officer friendly" and no one dared show them any disrespect. But now men seek to kill them just because they are policemen! Our alabaster streets no longer exist as they are stained with blood.

What has brought about this change? How is it that we have become afraid of our own neighbors? What is the explanation for this terrible malady? We are told in Psalm 9:17, "The wicked shall be turned into hell, and all the nations that forget God." We have become a nation that has removed God from our schools. We have removed Him from the public square. The Sabbath has been profaned, and industry and recreation have led the way in profaning the Sabbath. As for the nation, she is a cut flower and soon will pass away as other great empires of the past. With the loss of the Sabbath, there is the loss of the consciousness of God which leads to the dissolution of man. America is severed from her roots. She will soon bow her head and give up the ghost, that is, unless she returns to the Lord Who made her great. She must begin by remembering the Sabbath day to keep it holy. The Sabbath was made for man!

Awake! Awake my soul arise
And greet the God of earth and skies
Come with song and praises too,
That His blessings may fall on you!

Forsake Thou not this Holy Day!
From all thy labors come away!
Forbid thy soul should die in you.
O Seek the Lord and be renewed!

CHAPTER 6

What Day Is the Sabbath Day?

The question which is often brought up in addressing the doctrine of the Sabbath is, "On which day is the Sabbath to be observed?" It is apparent from both Scripture and the testimony from historical records that man is obligated to come apart one day in seven, ceasing from all his labors. He is to draw nigh to his Creator. But which day of the seven is to be hallowed? On what day of the week is the Sabbath to be observed?

Some are persuaded that the Sabbath is to be observed on the seventh day of the week. Saturday is said to be the Sabbath day which was ordained from the creation of the world. It is without question that the Sabbath was ordained and observed on the seventh day from the creation of the world. The evidences of this are overwhelming. (These evidences were set forth in the previous chapter.) Many, therefore, observe the Sabbath on the seventh day which is Saturday, and as for others, for the most part, they are in doubt.

Those who hold to the position of a Saturday Sabbath observance are not only the Jews but also Seventh Day Baptists and Seventh Day Adventists. They also affirm that our Lord rested on the seventh day from all His works from the Creation of the world, and we are to do the same in following His example. This is what the fourth commandment mandates. The seventh day is none other than Saturday. But is this position right?

Then there are the Muslims who observe the Sabbath on Friday. They argue that God rested on Friday from all His work of creation. However, it is not always realized that the Muslim weekly holy day is essentially different from the Jewish or the Christian Sabbath observance. For the Muslims, the Sabbath is not at all a day of rest but one of obligatory public worship, held at noon, the most characteristic part of which is a sermon consisting of two sections. However, it is on Friday that the Muslims come apart, recognizing it to be the holy day which all men are obliged to observe.

Those in professing Christendom strongly affirm that the first day of the week is the Sabbath. However, they refer to the Sabbath as the Lord's Day because it was on the first day of the week that our Lord Jesus was bodily raised from the grave. Hence, the Christian Sabbath is observed on the first day of the week in commemoration of the resurrection of our Lord. On this day, Christians cease from their labors and draw near to the Lord in worship.

Therefore, the great controversy that exists between the Christian community and collectively, the Jews, the Seventh Day Baptists, and the Seventh Day Adventists centers upon what day in the week is to be hallowed. The Muslim Sabbath is seldom if ever taken into consideration as it was not practiced until the time of Mohammad. This practice came into existence sometime in the seventh century. As for Christians, they are not concerned with the Muslim holy day.

There are those who question if the Seventh Day Baptists, the Seventh Day Adventists, and the Jewish community are right in holding to a Saturday observance of the Sabbath. The question before us is whether we are to observe the Sabbath on Saturday or on Sunday? Those who hold to a Saturday Sabbath present some considerable arguments that should be addressed.

For example, those who hold to the Sabbath being on Saturday defend their position from the New Testament as well as from the Old Testament. One argument presented is that our Lord observed the Sabbath on Saturday. No one can read the gospels and fail to perceive that it was His custom to go up to the synagogue and worship on the Sabbath which was the seventh day. Christians who observe Sunday as the Lord's Day do not argue that point but only because the old economy had not yet passed away.

Another argument states that the apostle Paul and Silas observed the Sabbath on Saturday and not on the first day of the week. For example, Acts 17:2-3 says,

> And Paul, as his manner was, went in unto them,
> and three sabbath days reasoned with them out of the
> Scriptures, Opening and alleging, that Christ must
> needs have suffered, and risen again from the dead; and
> that this Jesus, whom I preach unto you, is Christ.

Therefore, if the Sabbath were changed to Sunday, why did Paul enter into the synagogue of the Jews on the Sabbath day? Then to confuse the issue even more, some claim that it was Constantine who officially made Sunday the Sabbath.

To answer these objections, certain things should be understood. When the apostles evangelized among the Gentiles, they began by first going to the Jews. In Romans 1:16 we read, "For I am not ashamed of the gospel of Christ: for it is the power of God unto salvation to every one that believeth; to the Jew first, and also to the Greek." Therefore, it should be of no surprise to anyone that the apostles went to the synagogues on Saturday to evangelize the Jews.

If they had gone on the first day of the week to preach the gospel to the Jews, no one would have been there.

Nevertheless, it is strongly argued that nowhere in the New Testament do we have an explicit mandate stating that the saints are to worship on Sunday. Nowhere does it state that the Sabbath was transferred from the seventh day to the first day of the week. This is certainly true. There is not a single mandate given where we are to observe the Sabbath on the first day of the week.

However, there are incidentals that cannot be ignored. What makes these incidentals so pronounced is that they are just that, incidentals! There was no commandment given, yet this was and is the universal practice by the Church. Those in the early Church observed every Lord's Day as the Sabbath. This in itself is arresting. This is especially arresting since the early Church was greatly comprised of Jews. All the apostles were Jews, yet we find them coming apart on the first day of the week to worship.

This is an undeniable fact. This practice was universally accepted by the early Christian community throughout the known world. The early saints, without question, observed the Sabbath on the first day of the week. They referred to it as the Lord's Day. What makes this so astounding is that we do not have a specific commandment that mandates this practice. We do not find a commandment anywhere commanding the saints to observe the Sabbath on the first day of the week. Nevertheless, they did just that. This in itself is a marvel!

There is a remarkable incidental in 1 Corinthians 16:1-2. There we read of the apostle Paul giving instructions to the churches at Corinth in regard to taking up an offering for the impoverished Hebrew brethren. He writes,

> Now concerning the collection for the saints, as I have given
> order to the churches of Galatia, even so do ye. Upon the first
> day of the week let every one of you lay by him in store, as God
> hath prospered him, that there be no gatherings when I come.

The reader should observe that Paul instructed the Church in Corinth to take up this offering for the suffering saints on the first day of the week. Why? We are told that this practice was preferred so that there would be no need to gather together on any other day. If they had gathered together on Saturday, then what was said would make no sense. It is apparent, then, that they did not gather together on the seventh day of the week but rather on the first day. They did this because the Christian Sabbath observance was not on Saturday but on Sunday. Therefore, the day when they gathered to worship was the day they were to take up this collection for the suffering saints in Israel.

However, there is much more said by the apostle that is equally arresting. In the first verse of 1 Corinthians 16, Paul tells us that he had given these very same instructions to the churches in Galatia. Notice the word "churches" and not "church." What are we to gather from this? We are to gather that the churches universally observed the Sabbath on the first day of the week. Furthermore, the early Church observed the Sabbath on the first day of the week in Corinth, which is in Europe, and in Galatia, which is in Asia. Thus, on these two predominant continents, the saints universally observed the Sabbath on the first day of the week.

Another passage which is equally as arresting is found in Acts 20: 6-7. Luke, in recording his journey with Paul, writes,

> And we sailed away from Philippi after the days of unleavened
> bread, and came unto them to Troas in five days; where
> we abode seven days. And <u>upon the first day of the week,</u>

when the disciples came together to break bread, Paul preached unto them, ready to depart on the morrow; and continued his speech until midnight. (emphasis added)

Notice that Luke through the Holy Spirit carefully chronicles Paul's journey. He says that they sailed after the days of unleavened bread, the Passover, from Philippi to Troas. The journey took five days. Then he said that they spent seven days with the brethren at Troas. This is one week. It is important that we grasp this essential detail. After that, we read that on the first day of the week, the disciples came together and broke bread, and Paul preached unto them. Observe when they assembled. They did not assemble on Saturday but rather on Sunday. It was on the first day of the week. These incidentals are most pronounced as they give us a revelation of the practices of the early Church in regard to the observance of the Sabbath.

The words "and upon the first day of the week when the disciples came together" reveals that this was their customary practice. This gathering was not an exception. The word "when" is revealing. We are told that it was on this day "when" the saints gathered together. It was on this day that they observed the Sabbath.

Now if the Christians observed the Sabbath on Saturday, as many assert, then what shall we make of what is said? In the passages mentioned above, it is understood that the saints universally assembled on the first day of the week. This is also sanctioned by the Apostle Paul because the Sabbath is to be observed on the first day of the week. This is an indisputable fact. Nowhere in the Holy Record do we find the saints ever assembling on any other day for worship except Sunday, or what we call the Lord's Day. (The Ebonites which were Jewish quasi Christians are an exception. They accepted Jesus as the Messiah but denied His deity. These are not Christians.)

The question with which we are now faced is how did such a drastic transition come about? Something traumatic had to happen to make this radical change. Consider that from the creation of the world until the time of the New Testament church, the Sabbath was always observed on Saturday. Something unspeakable and astounding had to take place to alter that practice. And that was the bodily resurrection of our Lord Jesus from the grave! That momentous event took place on the first day of the week. This was the most colossal event of all time! It ushered in a new dispensation. The shadows passed away as the fulfillment of them had come to pass through the resurrection of our Lord Jesus Christ.

The observance of the Sabbath on the first day of the week is an irrefutable witness to this day of the resurrection of our Lord. For what could ever avail to move the saints to make such a radical change of that which was practiced from the foundation of the world? It was something astounding and marvelous--the resurrection of our Lord when He victoriously conquered death, hell, and the grave. It is such a wonder of wonders that the old economy had passed away which was but a shadow of better things to come. This truth cannot be overstressed. The saints rejoice with a great joy shouting, "...Alleluia: for the Lord God omnipotent reigneth" (Revelation 19:6).

But as traumatic as the resurrection of our Lord was, how was this transition made from Saturday to Sunday? We know that on the first day of the week, our Lord was raised from the dead (Matthew 28:1). What had then taken place was more than staggering. It was unbelievable until our Lord showed Himself to His disciples on several occasions. But even then they had to be instructed in order to make this radical change from a Saturday to a Sunday Sabbath. How were they instructed? Can it not be that it was by the appearances of our Lord to the disciples after His passion? It was on the first day of the week, after His passion, that our Lord appeared unto his disciples.

In John 20:1, we read that it was on the first day of the week that Mary Magdalene came to the sepulcher seeking our Lord. But He was not there. He had risen. Thus weeping, she thought that someone had taken away His body. Our Lord suddenly revealed Himself to her. This appearance of our Lord was on the first day of the week.

Then in the same chapter in verse 19 we read,

> Then the same day at evening, being the first day of the week, when the doors were shut where the disciples were assembled for fear of the Jews, came Jesus and stood in the midst, and saith unto them, Peace be unto you.

Our Lord appeared to His disciples on that Sabbath day evening. Again, it is said that He revealed Himself to them on the first day of the week. It was not on Saturday because on Saturday, He was still in the tomb. However, on that first Lord's Day morn when He appeared to His disciples, there was one disciple missing. It was Thomas. No doubt the rest of the disciples ran to tell Thomas the good news, but when the disciples told Thomas that they had seen the Lord risen from the grave, he did not believe them.

Then in verse 26 of the same chapter, we read that the next Sunday, counting eight days from that very day, Thomas was with them. Our Lord then appeared to His disciples a second time with Thomas present. Thomas saw and believed and in His presence confessed Jesus "My Lord and my God" (John 20:28). This third appearance of our Lord was on the Lord's Day which is the first day of the week.

It is interesting that our Lord waited until the following Sunday to reveal Himself to Thomas. But what is arresting is that it was not on Saturday but on Sunday that our Lord was pleased to make Himself known to His disciples this second time. From the day of the resurrection of our Lord, the Sabbath was no longer to be observed on the seventh day of the week. Now the celebrated day is the Lord's Day. The very first day of the week is now observed as the Christian Sabbath.

It is also arresting that another momentous event took place on the first day of the week. It was the wonder of Pentecost. On that momentous day, our Lord poured out the Holy Spirit upon the saints. The Day of Pentecost is the fiftieth day following seven sevens, or seven Sabbaths (weeks). Thus, Pentecost fell on the Lord's Day which is the first day of the week. Again, the Christian Sabbath is punctuated by a colossal event which fell on the first day of the week. The church of our Lord Jesus Christ, in one respect, was born on that day. On that day, the people of God were filled with His Spirit!

Later, we read that our Lord revealed Himself to John on the Isle of Patmos. We are specifically told that it was on the first day of the week, or the Lord's Day (Revelation 1:10). This is no mere coincidence. Since that mighty act of God in raising our Lord Jesus Christ from the dead, a new economy was ushered in and the old vanished. We must not seek to cling to the shadows of things that were but rather cling to the promises of better things to come. We are to embrace the substance of that which was prophesied. This is the new creation which has taken place in Jesus Christ our Lord. The Church is a new creation indeed!

Throughout the annals of history, since the resurrection of our Lord Jesus Christ, the saints have always observed the Sabbath on the first day of the week. This is a period of over 2000 years! This is the everlasting witness to the world that Jesus Christ our Lord has indeed been raised from the dead. What other explanation can one give for such a radical change of Sabbath days? Keep in mind how the Sabbath was observed on the seventh day from the foundation of the world, and now in these last days, it is observed on the first day of the week. This is staggering. Again, the only explanation of this is that something earth shattering had to take place. And that momentous event that brought about this radical change was that Jesus Christ our Lord had been raised from the dead. He ever lives making intercession for His saints.

> Are we left, to ourselves to guess
> Which Day, God ordained for rest?
> By Word and Act, our God did show
> That which saints had come to know.

> On the First Day we come apart
> It's with worship we must start.
> Neither is this something new
> This was the same with Adam too!

CHAPTER 7

Does the Fourth Commandment Mandate a Saturday Observance?

Many are of the opinion that regardless of what is said, the fourth commandment mandates Saturday to be the Sabbath day. Saturday is, without question, the seventh day of the week. Therefore, to observe the Sabbath on Sunday and not on Saturday, one would think that this would be a direct violation of the fourth commandment. The fourth commandment clearly states:

> Remember the sabbath day, to keep it holy. Six days shalt thou labour, and do all thy work: But the seventh day is the sabbath of the Lord thy God: in it thou shalt not do any work, thou, nor thy son, nor thy daughter, thy manservant, nor thy maidservant, nor thy cattle, nor thy stranger that is within thy gates: For in six days the Lord made heaven and earth, the sea, and all that in them is, and rested the seventh day: wherefore the Lord blessed the sabbath day, and hallowed it (Exodus 20:8-11).

Hence, the day that God hallowed was the seventh day.

There is no dispute how the fourth commandment enjoins man. Neither should one seek to alter or negate what is said. The fourth commandment must stand unaltered. However, if we read the fourth commandment carefully, we will discover that no specific day is mentioned to be observed as the Sabbath. We do not have the cardinal number "seven" given but rather we have the consecutive number "seventh." The "seventh day" is only determined from where one begins counting. If we begin counting from Tuesday, then Monday would be the seventh day. If we begin counting from Saturday, then Friday would be the seventh day. As one can readily see, it depends upon what day of the week one begins counting in order to arrive at the seventh day.

What the fourth commandment mandates is that for one day in seven, we are to come apart and cease from our labors. We are to follow God's example Who created the earth in six days and rested on the seventh. We must acknowledge that no day is specified as the Sabbath. The particular day which is to be observed as the Sabbath cannot be determined by reading the fourth commandment. If we are to determine what day is to be observed as the Sabbath, we have to look elsewhere in the Holy Scriptures.

As one can readily see, it would be wrong to assume that the fourth commandment specifies Saturday to be the day on which the Sabbath is to be observed. The fourth commandment only states that we are to work six days, and the seventh day we come apart and rest. The cardinal number "seven" is nowhere to be found in this divine mandate. However, the consecutive number "seventh" is mentioned twice. Let us not confuse a consecutive "seventh" with the cardinal number "seven."

This is not to deny that man, from the Creation of the world, observed Saturday as the Sabbath. This was conclusively proven in the former chapters. Neither is it to be denied that the seventh day of Creation is what we refer to as a Sabbath day as stated in many languages of the world. No one would deny this. Saturday was without question understood to be the Sabbath day under the old economy. Universally speaking, man throughout the world acknowledged Saturday as the Sabbath. This was true before the Flood as well as after the Flood.

Nevertheless, at the same time it remains, no matter how hard one studies the fourth commandment, that no one can determine which day is to be observed as the Sabbath day. No specific day is mentioned in the fourth commandment. The fourth commandment states that on one day in seven, we are to cease from all labor and hallow the Sabbath day. But again, it does not tell us what day that is. Neither does it tell us where we are to begin counting our days. If we desire to know what day the Sabbath is to be observed, we must look elsewhere in the Scriptures.

God told Israel in Exodus chapter 12 that the beginning of months was to commence with their deliverance out of Egypt (Exodus 12:2). From that point in time, Israel began to count day one. It was at that moment in time they started their calendar. The calendar of Israel commenced with the day they were delivered out from under the bondage of Pharaoh. It began around the time of the Passover.

Then in the sixth verse of this same chapter, they were told that on the fourteenth day they were to kill the Passover lamb. This would be on their Sabbath as their Sabbath was on the seventh day of the week. Israel's Sabbath was in commemoration of their deliverance out of Egypt (Deuteronomy 5:15-16). What we should gather from all that is said is that Israel had to be taught what day to observe the Sabbath (Nehemiah 9:13-14).

However, even though the fourth commandment does not specify a certain day for the Sabbath, this does not mean that a person may randomly choose whatever day he desires to be his Sabbath, just as long as one day in seven is chosen. Banish such thoughts. As God taught Israel what day they were to observe the Sabbath, so God, in like manner, teaches us what day we are to observe the Sabbath. We have been taught that it is the first day of the week which is called the Lord's Day (Revelation 1:10).

When our Lord was raised from the dead He ushered in a new day, and we, in Him, have become a new creation. In 2 Corinthians 5:17 we read, "Therefore if any man be in Christ, he is a new creature: old things are passed away; behold, all things are become new." What a wonder! What a marvel! We have become a new creation in Christ Jesus, and with this new creation, we have entered into a new Sabbath which is on the first day of the week. This does not in any way contradict the fourth commandment, but rather it magnifies it.

Lastly, the divine intent from the Creation of the world is again realized. The very first day of Adam's existence was a Sabbath. Adam began with worship and then work. So it is with the saints who have become a new creation in Christ Jesus. How wonderfully this is stated in 1 Corinthians 15:22: "For as in Adam all die, even so in Christ shall all be made alive"! All things now become new! Ah! We begin with worship! Man again begins with worship as it was intended from the creation of the world! And as for the Fourth Commandment, it is magnified!

> Jesus Christ our exalted Head
> He is risen from the dead!
> On the Morn of that First Day
> All the shadows passed away!
>
> The blood, the fire and smoke too!
> These sacrifices will never do!
> They all pointed unto Him
> Who alone atones for sin.

Now there's a new Sabbath day
The former now has passed away.
On the First Day of the week
We come apart, His face to seek.

CHAPTER 8

How Is the Sabbath To Be Observed?

In the second chapter of Mark's Gospel, verses 27-28, our Lord made two arresting declarations in defense of His disciples. But also what He said was for the benefit of the Jews in order that they might understand how the Sabbath was to be observed. We should keep in mind that they were sincere in their jealousy of keeping the Sabbath holy but wrong in their understanding of how it was to be observed because they did not understand why God had ordained the Sabbath. All they seemed to know was that the Sabbath was to be observed lest the people should forget their God. But they did not know the Divine intent in ordaining one day in seven for man to cease from all his labors and draw nigh to God.

When it comes to the observance of the Sabbath, many of these Pharisees were thoroughly confused. What is alarming is that today we are as much confused as these Pharisees were if not more. Those Jews had been taught certain things concerning the Sabbath, and what they were taught, they, in turn, taught others. They failed to prayerfully seek the Lord to open their understanding so that they might come to know the Divine intent in ordaining the Sabbath. This is much like what many are experiencing today; indoctrination rather than education. Those in professing Christendom profess they believe the Bible, but do they know what it says? They have been merely indoctrinated to accept certain teachings and fail to realize what God commands! Is this not evident in that we have so many different denominations?

Nevertheless, we are aware that there is a difference between those religious leaders and many professing Christians of our day. The Pharisees at least understood that the Sabbath was to be observed. They understood that the Sabbath was to be hallowed. It was to be separated from all other days. Professing Christians, for the most part, are not aware of this as they work and recreate on the Sabbath. They are not conscious of being "Sabbath breakers." Their conscience in some respects has been seared. It is inconceivable to most that in being Sabbath breakers they are guilty of a capital crime. If one should exhort them to repent and keep the Sabbath day holy, they would accuse him of being a legalist! This is only mentioned that we might become conscious of how far we have departed from the truth.

Therefore, it would be good to pause and reflect upon the declaration our Lord made to those Pharisees concerning the Sabbath. What He said must be understood in the context of that which had just taken place. The Pharisees understood that the Sabbath was not to be profaned. They had before them the example of the man being stoned for gathering sticks on the Sabbath. They also had the bitter history of the purging of their nation for forgetting Jehovah. Therefore, they were very jealous when it came to the Sabbath. Sabbath breakers were to be put to death. This was not open for discussion.

Let us consider what had taken place as the disciples and our Lord were walking through a corn field. It just happened to be the Sabbath. Being hungry, the disciples were picking corn and eating it. The Pharisees, in seeing them, became alarmed. As they saw it, the disciples were guilty of profaning the Sabbath. However, these Pharisees moved with discretion. They did not take up stones to stone the disciples; neither did they reprimand them. Instead, they went to the disciples' Master and informed Him of what His disciples were doing. In their minds, what His disciples were doing was not lawful. It is commendable how they took the matter up with the disciples' Master and not with the disciples themselves. They came to our Lord for Him to correct them. This was indeed admirable on their part.

However, they were wrong that the disciples were in any way violating the fourth commandment. Our Lord was quick to inform the Pharisees of that. He revealed something to them that they failed to grasp. He said, "…The sabbath was made for man, and not man for the sabbath" (Mark 2:27).

This is the underlying principle. The Sabbath was instituted for man's good. It was never meant to be a yoke upon his neck. This principle should have been understood as it was made for man from the foundation of the world. God, Who is "The Good," only ordains that which is good. God from the very beginning ordained the Sabbath which is good for the good of all humanity. Are you, dear reader, aware of this?

The purpose of the Sabbath has never been altered from the very day it was instituted. It was this fundamental principle that those poor Jews failed to grasp. They somehow failed to perceive that the Sabbath was made for the good of humanity. But we cannot rail upon them since all humanity, for the most part, has forgotten the necessity of Sabbath observance. If man understood this fundamental principle, then he would not profane the Sabbath nor would he oppose this divine mandate. Rather, he would jealously embrace it, understanding it was ordained for his benefit.

One may inquire why the man who picked up sticks on the Sabbath was stoned, yet the disciples who plucked corn on the Sabbath day were justified. Plucking corn and eating it on the Sabbath were surely an encroachment upon the fourth commandment. Then, what is the difference between the two acts? Or was there just an exception made for the disciples?

Again, we must keep in mind that Moses knew the letter as well as the spirit of the Law. This was why he inquired of the Lord what to do with the man picking up sticks. He knew what the man did, and he knew that the Sabbath was to be observed. But what he did not know was the reason or the motive of this man's heart. Therefore, he inquired of God, who knows the hearts of all men, what should be done with him. What one should keep in mind is that our Lord, who defended the disciples, is the same Lord Who gave the verdict to put the man to death for gathering sticks on the Sabbath. We know that there are no contradictions in Him because God changes not. "Jesus Christ the same yesterday, and to day, and for ever" (Hebrews 13:8).

With that, let us consider the illustration our Lord used to justify the disciples' actions. He gives an example drawn from 1 Samuel 21:1ff. In this passage, our Lord speaks of David and his men eating the show bread which was only to be eaten by the priests. They were hungry since they had not eaten anything for days. Thus, Ahimelech, the priest, gave David and his men the show bread to eat. In so doing, he never violated the Law of God. Keep in mind, the Law of God is made for our good; it should never be thought of as oppressive. (This is true of all the laws of God.)

Now what is our Lord emphasizing? He is emphasizing that the Sabbath was made for man. There is a far more graphic example of this truth given in John chapter five. Our Lord healed a man, who was infirmed for 38 years, on the Sabbath day. This had angered the Jews. They prohibited any kind of work on the Sabbath. But what they failed to realize was that this man in his condition was in sheer misery in need of deliverance. Surely, they should have understood that good works were not to be denied on the Sabbath.

In John 7:23, our Lord exposes the Pharisees' hypocrisy saying, "**If a man on the sabbath day receive circumcision, that the law of Moses should not be broken; are ye angry at me, because I have made a man every whit whole on the sabbath day?**" In other words, our Lord is emphasizing that certain works were permissible on the Sabbath, a fact that should have been understood in the Divine intent in creating the Sabbath. **It was made for man.** God loves us and desires the best for us. Our Lord never violated the fourth commandment by doing good works on the Sabbath.

A similar argument was presented when He made a lady whole on the Sabbath who had an infirmity for 18 years. This time he used a different illustration to justify good works on the Sabbath. He said,

> **...Thou hypocrite, doth not each one of you on the sabbath loose his ox or his ass from the stall, and lead him away to watering? And ought not this woman, being a daughter of Abraham, whom Satan hath bound, lo, these eighteen years, be loosed from this bond on the sabbath day?** (Luke 13:15-16).

One must also consider the man whose hand was withered. In Luke 6:9, our Lord, looking upon the Pharisees, asked, "**...Is it lawful on the sabbath days to do good, or to do evil? to save life, or to destroy it?**" They held their peace. Then our Lord healed the man, and they moved in anger and sought to put Him to death. His question to them was actually an affirmation that doing good works on the Sabbath is lawful.

Therefore, from these example and others like them, it should readily be understood that good works are permissible on the Sabbath day. Though the fourth commandment admonishes us not to do any work on the Sabbath, it is understood that good works and works of necessity are allowed and are not to be excluded. Nevertheless, it is understood that we cease from all secular works on the Sabbath. We are not to keep right on working seven days a week, profaning the Sabbath. We are to come apart one day of seven as we are commanded. But observing the Sabbath never gives place for idleness. Observe the life of our Lord Jesus. Also, consider the question He asked of those who sought His life, "Which of you convinceth me of sin" (John 8:46). Our Lord was sinless!

In John 5:17, our Lord said something staggering to those Jews that they should not have failed to understand. He said, "**...My Father worketh hitherto, and I work.**" Although Genesis says that God ceased from all of His work on the Sabbath, He had not ceased from His works in sustaining, keeping, and preserving His creation. The Father is continually working, and so is our Lord Jesus Christ. We are told that all things consist by Him (Colossians 1:17). If God ceased keeping His creation, then everything would collapse. What our Lord emphatically stated was that He and the Father are never idle. They are continually working. These works are works of necessity.

For example, the rancher's responsibility is to feed his cattle. Of course, he would try to make provisions for them on the previous day. "A righteous man regardeth the life of his beast: but the tender mercies of the wicked are cruel." (Proverbs 12:10) It would be cruel to ignore them because it is the Sabbath. If one works in a hospital, it would be wrong to walk away and forsake those infirmed souls on the Sabbath day. Also consider the necessity of policemen and firemen to work on the Sabbath. As anyone can readily see, it is essential to have some men on duty. The same is true of the military.

As for pharmacists, at one time they would close on the Lord's Day, and if anyone needed a prescription filled, they would open up their store and fill the prescription and then close the door and go home. Works of mercy, works of necessity—these were never meant to be excluded. This was something that the Pharisees failed to understand even though they themselves circumcised on the Sabbath (John 7:23).

As for the disciples plucking and eating corn, they were hungry. In passing through a corn field, they were allowed by law to pick the corn and eat it, which they did. In doing so, they were doing a work of necessity. They needed to be fed, and mercy says to feed them. Therefore, our Lord said they were guiltless, not Sabbath breakers. If these Pharisees understood that God loved mercy and not sacrifice, then they would not have condemned the guiltless (Matthew 12:7).

Nevertheless, there is the need for a word of caution. The Sabbath is not a time to go fishing. Neither is it a day to go golfing. Nor is it a day to go to a ball game or go shopping. There is not even to be any unnecessary traveling on the Sabbath. The Sabbath must not be profaned. But if a person breaks down on the road and needs help, we are to help him. We do not leave him stranded and say, "You will have to wait until tomorrow for me to help you pull your ox out of the ditch because this is the Sabbath."

In conversing with an orthodox Jew concerning the Sabbath, he mentioned that they do not even light a fire on the Sabbath day. I understand where they come from. In Exodus 35:3, our Lord clearly commanded, **"Ye shall kindle no fire throughout your habitations upon the sabbath day."** As we have stated earlier, neither the Babylonians nor the Assyrians kindled a fire on the Sabbath. So I asked this man, "How do you warm up your food?" He answered, "We leave a burner on all night." He was sensitive to the divine mandate.

In the past, Christians did all their cooking on Saturday and just warmed it on the Lord's Day. My personal habit has been the same. There is no "fire" to kindle today as there once was. We just turn on the stove and the fire is there. In the past, our forefathers did all the cooking on Saturday and just warmed it on the Lord's Day. These examples should remind us to be careful to observe the Lord's Day with reverence.

However, one should understand that works of necessity and helping those in need is never a violation of the Sabbath. We must keep in mind that the Sabbath was made for our good. Our Lord had demonstrated this for us time and time again. Are we not commanded to follow in His steps? Yet at the same time, there is a word of caution: Beware of profaning the Sabbath! Beware!

Following our Lord's clear declaration that the Sabbath was made for man, He made another startling declaration. What He said should have arrested His hearers. He said, "Therefore the Son of man is Lord also of the sabbath" (Mark 2:28). Did those Pharisees understand what He said? One wonders if the professing Christian community understands those arresting words. "Therefore the Son of man is Lord also of the sabbath"

From these words which the Lord spoke, we can clearly understand that Jesus Christ was the One Who, after creating all things, instituted the Sabbath. He Who spoke is God. These Pharisees at that time did not comprehend what He had said. If they did, they would have either stoned Him or fallen on their faces before Him. But John the apostle understood when he later wrote,

In the beginning was the Word, and the Word was with God, and the Word was God. The same was in the beginning with God. <u>All things were made by him; and without him was not any thing made that was made</u> (John 1:1-3). (emphasis added)

It was our Lord Jesus Who created all things. After creating all things, He rested on the seventh day. It was our Lord Jesus Who instituted the Sabbath. Our Lord Jesus is God manifested in the flesh (1 Timothy 3:16).

Because our Lord Jesus created the Sabbath for man, He alone can rightly interpret how it is to be observed. No one can better interpret the Sabbath, and how we should observe it, than He Who instituted it. The Pharisees looked to themselves and their scholars to interpret the Sabbath for themselves and how it was to be observed. To this day, man has not changed, as he also looks to men to tell him how to observe or not to observe the Sabbath. But if one desires to know anything concerning Sabbath observance, it would be best to inquire of Him Who instituted it. He is the Lord of the Sabbath. He is the One we seek to guide us in all truth. He is the One Who shall judge the world in righteousness. Let us follow His example.

Since the Sabbath was made for man, then the Sabbath should be a delight. It is meant to be a delight. Was it not instituted for our good? Therefore, let us heed the exhortation:

> **If thou turn away thy foot from the sabbath, from doing thy pleasure on my holy day; and call the sabbath a delight, the holy of the LORD, honourable; and shalt honour him, not doing thine own ways, nor finding thine own pleasure, nor speaking thine own words: Then shalt thou delight thyself in the LORD; and I will cause thee to ride upon the high places of the earth, and feed thee with the heritage of Jacob thy father: for the mouth of the LORD hath spoken it** (Isaiah 58:13-14).

It is obvious today that men do not call the Sabbath a delight; even professing believers are of the same mind as the world. This is the reason the nation is being destroyed. We have forgotten God. If the

Sabbath were a delight, our nation would be blessed. At one time, she was indeed blessed and was the most glorious nation in the entire world. She rode on the high places. But now she is on the verge of utter destruction. God has placed a blessing and a curse before us: a blessing if we obey and a curse if we disobey.

If one loves the Lord, then he will come apart and commune with God, feeding on His Word. One would love the fellowship with the saints and would separate himself from the world and find sweet rest for his soul. As for the praises and singing of hymns, this too would indeed be a delight. To the one who is not born again, the Sabbath is not a delight. But then he would not enjoy heaven either!

Lord Thou hast Created this Day
For us it is a blessing.
Thou art our Comfort and our Stay
We come before Thee with singing.

Now we're cumbered with many cares
Our bodies in toils are bending.
But Thou with our sorrows share
Always with us enabling.

We yearn for Thee to come and stay
We look for Thy appearing.
O Lord, may this be the Day!
In which praises shall be unending!

CHAPTER 9

Arguments and Answers Against Sabbath Observance

When it comes to the doctrine of the Sabbath, there are many who are thoroughly confused. They are not only confused, but they confuse others as well. There are sensitive saints who have been troubled with antinomian and dispensationalist teachings, as well as elements of Judaism. The battles in which we are presently engaged are the same as those with which the early Church had to contend. Certainly, we have the same enemy, the devil, who is a deceiver.

For example, there are those who teach that the Sabbath was instituted at Sinai, and it was only to be observed by the Jews. It is apparent that this is not true in light of the evidences that have been presented. However, there are many who stumble over passages such as Romans 14:5-6, Galatians 4:9-11, and Colossians 2:16-17. All of these passages should be carefully examined as they are often cited in refuting a Sabbath observance.

For example, in the Colossians passage we read, "Let no man therefore judge you in meat, or in drink, or in respect of an holyday, or of the new moon, or of the Sabbath days: Which are a shadow of things to come; but the body is of Christ." (Colossians 2:16-17) Thus, it is implied that the Sabbath observance had been annulled.

In considering the epistle to the Colossians as well as the epistle to the Galatians, and even portions of Romans, it is apparent that the apostle Paul was addressing particular problems that existed in these churches. He was correcting the heretical teachings of the Gnostics as well as those of the renegade Jews who were plaguing the churches with their false teachings. Although there were different forms of Gnosticism plaguing the churches, one thing they all had in common was their claim of possessing superior knowledge to that of the prophets and the apostles. The very word Gnostic comes from the Greek word γινωσκω (ginosko) which means "to know."

As for the saints in Colossae, they were plagued with a strange form of Gnosticism. This particular form of Gnosticism was a blending of Judaism with oriental teachings. There was a "will worship" which was a prideful humility. They also incorporated the worship of angels with the observance of Jewish feast days. In reading the epistle, it is readily seen how the apostle Paul was correcting many things, one of which was the observance of Sabbath days. Those various Sabbath days of the Jews, he pointed out, were no longer to be observed. They were but shadows of better things to come.

Note Colossians 2:15-16, "And having spoiled principalities and powers, he made a shew of them openly, triumphing over them in it. Let no man therefore judge you in meat, or in drink, or in respect of an holyday, or of the new moon, or of the sabbath days." The argument that we are no longer to observe the Sabbath is based upon the word "days," which Sabbath opponents argue is not in the original. In this text, the word "days" is italicized which indicates that the translators supplied this word in translating the Greek text into English. Therefore, some assert that the reading should be that we are no longer to observe the Sabbath. It is true that the word "days" is in italics, indicating that the translators supplied it. But what is ignored is that the definite article "the" is absent in the Greek which makes a tremendous difference in the interpretation of the text. It is quite clear that the apostle is not referring to the fourth commandment.

Also, the word "Sabbath" is in the plural in the original. Therefore, "sabbath days" is correctly understood as the word "Sabbaths" and not "Sabbath." "Sabbaths" in the plural is to be understood in the text but is often overlooked. If the Sabbath was no longer to be binding, then the Greek text would have read "the Sabbath" and not "Sabbaths." What we should realize is that there were various Sabbath days which the Jews observed. These Sabbath days were no longer to be observed because they were but shadows of better things to come. Thus, the word "days" is rightly supplied for clarity, making a distinction between those Sabbath days and the fourth commandment. In other words, the feasts of the Passover, Tabernacles, Atonement, and others were Sabbath days which are no longer to be observed. Again, these were but shadows of better things to come. This was what the apostle was addressing.

Those who are familiar with Judaism realize that the Jews observed many sabbaths. The feast days they observed commenced with a Sabbath and concluded with a Sabbath. These various feasts are collectively referred to as Sabbath days. The apostle asserts that these Sabbath days were no longer to be observed. At no time did the apostle challenge the fourth commandment. It is readily understood that there is a vast difference between observing "Sabbath days" and in observing the Sabbath.

As for the Galatians epistle, it is quite obvious the apostle was contending with apostate Jews who were seeking to bring the people into bondage by observing the "beggarly elements." This was the problem of the Ebonites who plagued the early Church. Even to this day, we have people seeking to bring us under the dietary law which is so pronounced with the Seventh Day Adventists.

In reflecting upon the Church in Rome, we discover that it was composed of both Jew and Gentile converts. Some of these Jews, as those with James, had a hard time letting go of their old customs. Thus, in regard to this problem in the Church, the apostle writes,

> He that regardeth the day, regardeth it unto the Lord;
> and he that regardeth not the day, to the Lord he doth
> not regard it. He that eateth, eateth to the Lord, for he
> giveth God thanks; and he that eateth not, to the Lord
> he eateth not, and giveth God thanks (Romans 14:6).

However, this has nothing to do with the fourth commandment. What he writes in the Roman epistle was in regard to those feast days and not with the fourth commandment. Elsewhere in this epistle, the apostle exalts the Law.

Then there are those who argue that our Lord Jesus is our rest, and therefore, we are not to observe the Sabbath day any longer. But what they assert is not true. It is twisting the Scriptures to make them say what they want them to say. Nevertheless, many have been mislead by their corrupt teaching. Therefore, it behooves us to pause and reflect upon Matthew 11:28-30. It reads,

> **Come unto me, all ye that labour and are heavy laden, and I
> will give you rest. Take my yoke upon you, and learn of me;
> for I am meek and lowly in heart: and ye shall find rest unto
> your souls. For my yoke is easy, and my burden is light.**

Thus, twice over it affirms that our Lord Jesus is our "rest." Some infer that Jesus Christ, being our rest, is our Sabbath. But that is not what our Lord implies.

At no time does our Lord ever say He is our Sabbath. The word "rest" in our text is "αναπαυσιν" (anapausin) which is rightly translated "I will give you rest." There is no way in rightly handling the sacred Scriptures that one can make "rest" to mean "Sabbath" although the Sabbath is a rest of the heart. Furthermore, all men, sinners and saints alike, are to observe the Sabbath. However, only those who have come in repentance and faith to Christ know anything of the rest of which our Lord speaks in Matthew 11:28-30. How wrong it is to speak of this rest in Christ to be our Sabbath. There is a great deal of difference between "αναπαυσιν" (anapausin) and "Sabatismos" (a Sabbath keeping).

What one should understand in the above passage is that all men who are outside of Christ are restless. Although they seek rest, they will never find it except in our Lord Jesus Christ. And only those who come by faith find this rest that our Lord offers to all men. But as for the Sabbath, all humanity is to observe it—the saved as well as the lost.

There is one more argument that should be addressed that seeks to do away not only with the Sabbath but also with the entire law. The argument begins with stating that the reason the man was stoned for taking up sticks on the Sabbath was because he was under the Law. The argument continues with stating that we are now under grace, and therefore, we are not to be disciplined for violating the Sabbath. Furthermore, it is implied that we are no longer obligated to obey the Law. To state the argument's affirmation more plainly, we are no longer obligated to obey the Lord. This is what is actually implied when it is said we are not obliged to obey the Law. Of course, this is utter nonsense!

Consider Luke 6:46 in light of the above argument: "And why call ye me, Lord, Lord, and do not the things which I say?"

Taking the argument a step further, many argue from the standpoint that we are no longer under the Law but under grace, a teaching which reveals that they do not know what they affirm. They cite the woman taken in adultery in the eighth chapter of John. Those holding to this argument say that our Lord did not have her stoned because we are now under grace and not under the Law. We know the Law demands that she was to be put to death. This argument holds that our Lord put away the Law and showed her grace. He said, "Neither do I condemn thee: go, and sin no more" (John 8:11).

Two things are overlooked in citing this passage in favor of putting away the Law. First, our Lord never said that the Law was put away. He said, "He that is without sin among you, let him first cast a stone at her" (John 8:7). He never said the Law was nullified. However, only those with clean hands who were without sin were to cast stones. The reason the sentence was not carried out was because there were no qualified executioners. Have we not read in **Romans 3:23 that "all have sinned, and come short of the glory of God"**? And again in **Romans 5:12, "Wherefore, as by one man sin entered into the world, and death by sin; and so death passed upon all men, for that all have sinned."** All men are under the sentence of condemnation until they come to Christ.

Why didn't our Lord have her put to death? He is sinless. To ask another question, why didn't our Lord put them all to death as the wages of sin is death? (Romans 6:23) It is because the mission of our Lord was not to condemn the world but that the world through Him might be saved (John 3:17). He came to save sinners and not damn them to hell. Even suffering on the cross, He prayed, "Father, forgive them; for they know not what they do" (Luke 23:34).

However, there is **"appointed a day, in the which he will judge the world in righteousness" (Acts 17:31).** In that day, **"the fearful, and unbelieving, and the abominable, and murderers,**

and whoremongers, and sorcerers, and idolaters, and all liars, shall have their part in the lake which burneth with fire and brimstone: which is the second death" (Revelation 21:8). What will these law breakers say in that day? Lord! Lord! Were we not under grace? Grace does not allow us to sin; rather, it makes us a new creation (2 Corinthians 5:17). So much for this perversion of grace that is so popular in this day of apostasy.

When we come to Hebrews 4:9, we read, "There remaineth therefore a rest to the people of God." The word "rest" in the Greek ("Σαββατισμος") is "Sabbatismos" or a "Sabbath keeping." We are plainly told that there remains yet to this day a Sabbath keeping for the people of God. This not only concerns the present times in which we live but also points to that eternal Sabbath which is to come. The doctrine of the Sabbath grows as we come to realize that in Heaven we shall enjoy the eternal Sabbath. Thus, the doctrine of the Sabbath never changes. It grows as one follows the teaching throughout the Scriptures. Therefore, if one finds the observance of the Sabbath oppressive, then such would definitely not like heaven, for in Heaven, there is one eternal Sabbath for the people of God.

Oh Blessed Holy Sabbath day
That calls me from this world away.
And from all its clamorous noise
Unto God's eternal joys

And with the breaking of this day
Unto Christ I fly away
And here I take my sweet repose
In Christ Who died and then arose.

CHAPTER 10

Sabbath Observance
Should Be Enforced

It may sound strange that laws should be legislated, making all commerce and entertainment to cease on the Sabbath. To some this may seem to be unattainable as we are caught up in a highly industrialized and complex economic system. It is believed that in these modern times these Sabbath laws cannot possibly be enacted or would be impractical. Also, some argue that there is a separation between the Church and State that would forbid such legislation. Hence, to legislate Sabbath Laws, it is argued that they would be contrary to our Constitution. However, if we pause and consider the above arguments, none of these objections are plausible.

First, let us consider the effect of Sabbath laws on a country's economic system. In Israel, everything closes down on Saturday, which is the day they observe as their Sabbath. Even the elevators stop on every floor eliminating the need to press buttons to arrive at one's desired destination.[11] All commerce also comes to a halt one day in seven. What should be taken into consideration is that Israel is a nation that is constantly threatened by the surrounding nations seeking to annihilate her. The constant cry of these nations is "death

---

[11] "Shabbat Elevator." Wikipedia.org.

to Israel." Yet one day in seven, everything comes to a halt. Hence, the notion that, in times such as these, such laws are unreasonable is not true.

Industrialization aside, the other argument presented is that our own country has a separation of church and State. The term "separation between church and State" is a euphemism for separation of Christianity from the state. Such a separation is a myth. One cannot read the Declaration of Independence and fail to realize that the rights that we have are only those which are endowed to us by our Creator. The idea of human rights is not found in our Constitution. This noxious weed sprang up out of Hell and is nurtured by the United Nations.

What is of interest is that Thomas Jefferson, as well as John Adams and others, asked John Knox Witherspoon, a Scottish Presbyterian preacher and president of Princeton College (a Christian College at the time [12]), to edit the Declaration of Independence before it was presented to Congress. It was Witherspoon who inserted those words, "endowed by their Creator with certain unalienable Rights, that among these are Life, Liberty and the pursuit of Happiness." In other words, we do not have a right to sin.[13]

As for the men drafting the Constitution in that First Continental Congress, it appeared that all their efforts were in vain. The convention was in such disarray that delegates were fighting among themselves. After several days of dissension and strife, everyone was about to give up and go home. It was then that Benjamin Franklin took the floor and spoke saying,

---

[12] https://en.wikipedia.org/wiki/History_of_Princeton_University
[13] Rick Santorum, *American Patriots* (Carol Stream IL: Tyndale House Publishers house, 2007), 117.

> The Longer I live, the more convincing proofs I see of
> this truth, that God governs in the Affairs of men. And if
> a sparrow cannot fall to the ground without notice, is it
> probable that an empire can rise without His aid?.....I believe
> that without His concurring aid we shall not succeed in this
> political building no better than the builders of Babel.[14]

Franklin then called for Congress to deliberate and give themselves to three days of fasting, prayer, and preaching. So they did and came back in an entirely different spirit, putting together the greatest Constitution the world had ever seen. No constitution of any nation in the history of mankind has lasted as long as the one drawn up in that First Constitutional Convention.

It is interesting that the first speaker to address the congressional body during those three days was the Presbyterian preacher, John Witherspoon. He warned,

> Unless you are united to him (The Lord) by a lively
> faith, not the resentment of a haughty monarch, the
> word of divine justice hangs over you, and the fullness
> of divine vengeance shall speedily overtake you.[15]

At the birth of the nation, there was never the thought of separating the "Church" (Christianity) from the State. Never!

Furthermore, what shall we make of George Washington's farewell address? He made it clear that religion was essential in order to ensure the perpetuity of the Republic. In addressing the nation, he said,

---

[14] Nelson Beecher Keyes, *Ben Franklin: An Affectionate Portrait* (Garden City, NY: Hanover House, 1956), 282.

[15] (Santorum, *American Patriot*, 118)

Of all the dispositions and habits which lead to political prosperity, religion and morality are indispensable supports. In vain would that man claim the tribute of patriotism, who should labor to subvert these great pillars of human happiness, these firmest props of the duties of men and citizens....Let it simply be asked: Where is the security for property, for reputation, for life, if the sense of religious obligation desert the oaths which are the instruments of investigation in courts of justice? And let us with caution indulge the supposition that morality can be maintained without religion. Whatever may be conceded to the influence of refined education on minds or peculiar structure, reason and experience both forbid us to expect that national morality can prevail in exclusion of religious principle.[16]

He went on to say,

It is substantially true that virtue or morality is a necessary spring of popular government. The rule, indeed, extends with more or less force to every species of free government. Who that is a sincere friend to it can look with indifference upon attempts to shake the foundation of the fabric?[17]

Our Founders well documented the fact that our country, which is founded upon the government of the people, by the people, and for the people, cannot stand or continue without morality. Also, it is impossible to have morality without Christianity. Therefore, to argue separation of church (Christianity) and State is a myth. To hold to such a position is to undermine the very Constitution that guarantees our freedoms. It will sever us from our roots and thus destroy our Republic!

---

[16] George Washington, *George Washington's Farewell Address* (Belford, MA: Applewood Books, 1993) 23-24.
[17] (Washington, *George Washington's Farewell Address*, 24)

In his farewell address, Washington goes on to say,

> Can it be that Providence (God) had not connected the permanent felicity of a nation with its virtue (Morality). The experiment, at least, is recommended by every sentiment which ennobles human nature. Alas! It is rendered impossible by its vices![18] (clarity added)

We should study George Washington's farewell address. If we would, then the amoral would never be entertained. Our Founders well understood that the amoral that our country has come to embrace is an enemy to our form of government. It is impossible to be a people of self-government when "human rights" replace the "**certain unalienable rights endowed to us by our Creator.**" The two cannot coexist as one stands in opposition to the other.

More may be said from Washington's farewell address to the nation, but said the examples given should be sufficient to impress the reader that the Founders of the nation never intended that there be a separation between Christianity and the State. The very foundation of our government of the people, by the people, and for the people implies that we must be a people who are able to govern ourselves. This is impossible apart from the human conscience held in check by the Word of God. Without a consciousness of God, the nation cannot continue. We cannot have morality without religion, which Washington and His peers understood. These were, in essence, the words of George Washington, the Founding Father of the nation.

If the Founding Fathers ever intended a separation of Christianity and the State, as it is interpreted today, then why was the Capitol the most religious building in the country? Early leaders of our country held church services there every Lord's Day. Both Jefferson and Madison faithfully attended those church services. Also, Jefferson appropriated government funds to finance the building of a church

---

[18] (Washington, *George Washington's Farewell Address*, 24)

for the Indians. Certainly, there was never the intent to separate the nation from Biblical Christianity.

If there were to be a separation of Christianity and the State as it is presently understood, then how do we explain John Jay's actions? John Jay was an American statesman, patriot, and diplomat and one of the Founding Fathers (1789–95). He was a lawyer who joined the New York Committee of Correspondence and organized opposition to British rule. He joined a conservative political faction that feared mob rule and sought to protect property rights and maintain the rule of law while resisting British violations of the colonists' rights. Jay served as the president of the first Continental Congress. During and after the American Revolution, he was an ambassador and negotiator of the Treaty of Paris, in which Great Britain recognized American independence. He was also the first Chief Justice of the United States. But few realize that he was also the founder of the American Bible Society. Does this sound like a man who held to the separation of Christianity and the State?

The Virginia colony, which was the most influential of the colonies, did not allow anyone to hold an office who did not hold to the Christian faith. For an example:

> Those who denied the Trinity or the inspiration of the
> Scriptures were to be disabled from all official civil capacities
> on the first offense and imprisoned on the second; those
> that absent themselves from divine services at the local
> parish churches were to be fined and perhaps whipped. [19]

This was not only true concerning Virginia from which the Founders promoted religious liberty, but this was also true of the other colonies.

---

[19] Michael Farris, *The History of Religious Liberty* (Green Forest, AR: Master Books, 2015), 331.

No one was to hold public office who denied the Trinity and the Holy Scriptures.

It is interesting that as late as 1961, a Maryland citizen was appointed to the office of Notary Public by the governor. Murphy states,

> He was refused a commission to serve because he would not declare his belief in God, the Supreme Court ruled that such a test for public office could not be enforced. It constitutionally invaded the appellant's freedom of belief and religion guaranteed by the First Amendment, and protected by the Fourteenth...[20]

This ruling was contrary to the Founders. It was contrary to the Rock upon which our Constitution rests, the Bible. This ruling was nothing more than legislating from the bench. Their ruling was contrary to the intent of the First Amendment.

It should arrest the reader that until 1961, there were states that barred people from office who did not believe in God! This was because we were a Christian nation. Because we were a nation founded upon Christian principles, there was no separation of Christianity and the State up to that time. This ruling coming down from the Warren Court was a devastating blow to our Constitution. It was contrary to the Supreme Court ruling of 1892 that America is a Christian nation.[21] However, later there followed many other rulings of the Court that ultimately removed God from our society. Gradually, they undermined the foundation of our Republic. Since then all of our institutions such as marriage, family, the home, law, and education began to crumble. How can they stand when the foundation is removed!

---

[20] Paul Murphy, *The Constitution in Crisis Times 1918-1969* (New York, San Francisco, London: Harper & Row, 1972), 391-392.

[21] https://en.wikipedia.org/wiki/Church_of_the_Holy_Trinity_v._United_States

President Kennedy weakly responded to the ruling that outraged the nation. He said:

> I think that it is important for us, if we are going to maintain our constitutional principle, that we support the Supreme Court decision, even though we may not agree with them. In addition, we have, in this case, a very easy remedy. And that is, to pray ourselves...[22]

If one reflects upon the various governments of the world up to this day, their institutions rest upon their religious beliefs. Communism holds to atheism, which is a religion. Christianity is a threat to atheism as well as all other religions including Hinduism, Islam, and Buddhism to name a few. In India the foundation of their government is Hinduism, and the Muslim countries hold to their religion handed down to them by Mohammad. Man is a religious creature and governs based on its religious beliefs.

In America in the 1950's, there was an underground swell of both communism and atheism which threatened the nation. By the 1960's, there was the great cry of Antidisestablishmentarianism. There was the movement of the youth to throw down and destroy this government, but they never said with what they would replace it. However, in order to destroy the nation, the foundation upon which it rested must first be removed. The Sabbath observance was one of the first things that had to go. It kept people conscious of their obligations to God.

In addressing this very matter, Paul Murphy wrote,

> Then in a series of Sunday Closing Law decisions, it held by varying majorities that state 'blue laws' violated neither the establishment of religion not the free exercise thereof, the third

---

[22] (Murphy, *The Constitution in Crisis Times 1918-1969*, 394)

of the cases Braunfeld v. Brown, it is especially appeared to take a lightly the contention that such laws infringed upon the free exercise of religion. Thus these Blue laws which were held by the majority of the states were struck down as unconstitutional.[23]

Until 1961, there were laws that prohibited commerce on the Sabbath. There was no such thing as the separation of Christianity and the State which is commonly voiced today. Our coinage still has our nation's motto, "In God We Trust," inscribed upon it. And as for our pledge allegiance to our flag, we pledge "one nation under God." Does this sound like there was ever the intent to separate God from our government?

From 1961, there has been an avalanche of laws coming down from the courts removing God, not only from the schools, but also from our society. The nation since then began to move away from the moral to the amoral which our Founding Fathers had cautioned us to avoid. However, these seeds of destruction were planted in the early 1800's.

Robert Winthrop, former speaker of the House and contemporary with John Quincy Adams and Daniel Webster, warned,

> Men, in a word, must necessarily be controlled, either
> by a power within them, or by a power without them;
> either by the word of God, or by the strong arm of
> man; either by the Bible, or by the bayonet.[24]

It may do for other countries and other governments to talk about the State supporting religion, but here under our free institutions, it is Christianity which must support the State.

---

[23] (Murphy, *The Constitution in Crisis Times 1918-1969*, 391-392)

[24] Winthrop, *Addresses and Speeches on Various Occasions*, (Boston: Little, Brown, and Company, 1852), 165-173.

Even Andrew Jackson in addressing the American Bible Society in 1845 said, "The Bible is the Rock on which our Republic rests." [25] The lives of all early Americans were in some degree shaped by the Holy Scriptures. This was because all of its institutions were influenced by the Holy Scriptures.

While visiting the United States, the French historian Alexis de Tocqueville was arrested how Church and State worked together. He wrote,

> Of all the countries of the world, America is surely the one in which the marriage bond is most respected, and in which people subscribe to the loftiest most just ideal of conjugal happiness......
> Americans are obliged to profess a certain public respect for Christian morality and equity, so that it is not easy for them to violate the Law when those laws stand in the way of their design. And even if they could overcome their own scruples, they would still be held in check by the scruples of their supports. No one in the United States has yet dared to propose the maxim that everything is permitted in the interest of society- a wicked maxim that seems to have been invented in an age of liberty to legitimize all tyrants of future...In the United States religion not only regulated mores but extends its empire over intelligence as well...Christianity therefore reigns without impediment. [26]

He went on to write,

> But I am certain that they believe it to be necessary for the preservation of the republican institutions. This is not the opinion of one class of citizens or one party but of the nation as a whole. One encounters it among people of every rank...Americans so

---

[25] http://providencefoundation.com/?page_id=888
[26] (de Tocqueville, *Democracy in America,* 337)

completely confounded Christianity with Liberty that it is almost impossible to induce them to think of one without the other. [27]

This was not merely the opinion of this historian but a conviction which came from observation. He later wrote,

Yet Sunday observance is still one of the things that the foreigners in America find most striking. In deed…social life comes to a halt on Saturday night. You can walk through the streets at a time that would seem to beckon mature men to business and youth to pleasure and find yourself quite alone. Not only is no one working, but no one seems to be alive. One hears neither the bustle of industry or the accents of pleasure or even the incessant hubbub of all large cities. Chains bar the way to churches, and only grudgingly do half-closed shutters allow even a ray of light to penetrate citizens' homes. From time to time one may just glimpse a solitary figure making his way across a desert intersection of an abandoned street. The next day, at day break, the rumble of carriages, the pounding of hammers, and the shouts of the people can again be heard. The city comes back to life. Restless crowds hasten to places of business and work… [28]

Our Founding Fathers understood the necessity of Sabbath observance when they gave us a Republic. Keyes relates the following dialogue between Benjamin Franklin and a friend who asked, "'Well Doctor, what have we got, a republic or a monarchy?' And the sagacious reply was, 'A republic—if you can keep it.'" [29] It is certain we cannot keep it without Biblical Christianity.

This was also the conviction of de Tocqueville. He enjoined the nation in writing, "I am so convinced that Christianity must be

---

[27] (de Tocqueville, *Democracy in America,* 338)
[28] (de Tocqueville, *Democracy in America,* 841)
[29] (Keyes, *Ben Franklin: An Affectionate Portrait,* 284-285)

maintained at all cost in the new democracies that I would rather chain priest inside their sanctuaries than allow to venture out." [30]

There are only two alternatives upon which our Republic may rest. One is atheism, a religion which she has begun to embrace. Accepting atheism means accepting the amoral, meaning there is no moral or something is immoral; thus, the unacceptable has become acceptable. No longer is anything considered unthinkable. A reasonable person should realize that no society can continue under such a delusion. She will destroy herself. However, this is the religion many in our country have come to embrace. In large part, our country has thrown off the faith of our fathers.

The second alternative is that we return to our roots, which is Biblical Christianity. If we do, we will make a distinction between the acceptable and the unacceptable. Ethics would again become a discipline taught, distinguishing between that which is right from that which is wrong. The Holy Bible would become our guiding light by which we would judge between right and wrong and thus insure "Domestic tranquility." To hold to the position of separation between Christianity and the State, as it is understood today, will only make us atheists. If we continue down this road of paganism, we shall surely be destroyed.

Where then do we begin? It is by observing the Sabbath. In observing the Sabbath, there is a profound consciousness of God in society. In coming away to meet with God one day in the week, we rediscover the old paths that lead to life, liberty, and the pursuit of happiness which is in Christ. Therefore, let us not ignore the exhortation, "Remember the Sabbath day, to keep it holy."

How blind! How blind can we be!
Having eyes and yet not see!

---

[30] (de Tocqueville, *Democracy in America*, 367)

Has our pride put out my eyes!
That we should follow these blind guides?

O Lord Thy salve, give unto us!
Anoint our eyes; in Thee to trust.
Draw us O Lord unto Thee!
And free us from earth's vanities!

APPLICATION

It is apparent that the institutions of our country are crumbling. The foundation, as earlier mentioned, has been removed. In desperation, one inquires, "What are we to do? How are we to meet the challenges that face us?" From 1918 to 1969, the Supreme Court, as Murphy has aptly pointed out, had gradually become a "liberal quasi legislative body." [31] The two Wars and the Great Depression had influenced the courts to become activists rather than jurists. Laws that were established to insure the perpetuity of the nation were and are overruled in favor of an individual's rights. This, in turn, has promoted anarchy. As one instance, the court ruled to remove prayer from the schools because one person was offended.

Later under freedom of speech, all manner of vileness surfaced. Pornography and other vile materials became lawful. Flag burning and disrespect for authority, in time, became the norm as a result of a false understanding of the First Amendment. Thus, the unthinkable ceased to be unthinkable. Presently, nothing is shocking. This is what happens when the foundation is removed. The single greatest document of our liberties is the Bible. But the nation has forgotten this and has launched out on uncharted seas without chart and compass.

In the 1960's, a nine-man court of unelected officials dictated to the nation what was and what was not lawful. Although rulings handed

---

[31] (Murphy, *The Constitution in Crisis Times 1918-1969*, xvii)

down by the High Court are rendered as "the opinion of the Court," their rulings are presently accepted as absolutes that none dare to challenge. These gods on Mount Olympus have spoken, and we must comply. The government of the people, by the people, and for the people no longer exists as nine unelected officials rule.

The power of the Supreme Court has presently been extended over the executive and legislative branches of our government. This is apparent when people are incarcerated if they do not comply with a ruling passed down from the High Court. For example, Kim Davis, Clerk of Rowan County, Kentucky, refused, upon her Christian beliefs, to issue marriage licenses to same sex couples. The U.S. District Court, upholding the Supreme Court ruling, ordered her to be incarcerated. The Court is taking greater power than that granted to them by the Founding Fathers. The Court was given no power. None! The court's rulings should be "the opinion of the court." The court was not intended to rule but merely render an opinion according to the Law.

As for the Christian community, it is very small. It is growing smaller with each passing day. The few and faithful find themselves hopeless in these dark, dismal days. To stand up against the giants of the land seems to be an impossible task. This is especially distressing when we are so few. However, when we read the Scriptures, time and again we discover that God's people, though they were few, had overcome horrendous odds. King Asa understood this when he prayed,

> **Lord, it is nothing with thee to help, whether with many, or with them that have no power: help us, O Lord our God; for we rest on thee, and in thy name we go against this multitude. O Lord, thou art our God; let no man prevail against thee** (2 Chronicles 14:11).

Asa did prevail, as it is nothing for God to use the things that are not, to bring to naught the things that are (1 Corinthians 1:28).

In 2 Chronicles 16:9 we read, "For the eyes of the Lord run to and fro throughout the whole earth, to shew himself strong in the behalf of them whose heart is perfect toward him." Our God is ready to work in behalf of those whose hearts are perfect before Him. To this day, God is looking for such people through whom He might work. This is apparent in times past, for when horrible opposition faced the people of God, they prayed, and our Lord sent great revivals restoring the nation. Even to this day, many are conscious of those revivals of the past and are exhorting the saints to pray. Their appeal is to fast and pray, and some are responding to the call. However, there is no sign from Heaven that God has heard. Why? How is it that God does not hear our tears and cries? Only one thing separates us from God, and that is sin.

Consider how Joshua won the victory over Jericho but soon thereafter lost the battle at Ai. Humbled and seized with fear, the people of Israel gave themselves to fasting and prayer. But the Lord would not hear them. Instead, our Lord rebuked them. He said, "Get thee up; wherefore liest thou thus upon thy face? Israel hath sinned" (Joshua 7:10-11). The accursed thing had to first be removed before our Lord would deliver. Therefore, before we can call upon the Lord, asking for His mercies, the accursed thing has to be removed. There is sin in the camp.

In confessing our sins, there is one grievous sin that is overlooked, which is profaning the Sabbath. This is a very grievous sin that must be confessed if we desire to have power with God. We must keep in mind that it is a capital offence to be a Sabbath-breaker. This becomes even more sobering when reading Isaiah 58:13-59:2. We must keep in mind that there are no chapter breaks in the Bible; these were added for our convenience.

The 58ᵗʰ and 59ᵗʰ chapters of Isaiah are critical in this hour. We are exhorted,

> If thou turn away thy foot from the sabbath, from doing thy
> pleasure on my holy day; and call the sabbath a delight, the holy

of the Lord, honourable; and shalt honour him, not doing thine own ways, nor finding thine own pleasure, nor speaking thine own words: Then shalt thou delight thyself in the Lord; and I will cause thee to ride upon the high places of the earth, and feed thee with the heritage of Jacob thy father: for the mouth of the Lord hath spoken it. Behold, the Lord's hand is not shortened, that it cannot save; neither his ear heavy, that it cannot hear: But your iniquities have separated between you and your God, and your sins have hid his face from you, that he will not hear.
(Isaiah 58:13 - 59:2)

How shall the nation return to her roots from which she has been severed if the Church fails to "Remember the Sabbath day, to keep it holy"? If Christians do not lead the way, who will?

O how glorious the nation glowed
When God's blessings on us bestowed.
On the Sabbath all was still
Men would pause to seek God's will.

But sin and greed in men did rise
To make on earth their paradise.
They first cast off the Sabbath day
And then from God we fell away.

Now the family has come apart
People trample on each other's heart.
Darkness darker grows each day,
Sense men from God have fallen away.

"Turn ye, Turn ye why will ye die"!
Unto us doeth our God cry!
Will we heed His loving call?
Will we turn or will we fall?

Appendix

Separation of Church and State as Defined in America

When men debate the separation of Church and State, the two sides have a different understanding of the term. This may be due to the fact that they have never seriously read the First Amendment. For example, the First Amendment clearly states that "Congress shall make no law respecting an establishment of religion, or prohibit the free exercise thereof." From the wording, it is clearly understood that Congress is prohibited from establishing a state church. But at the same time, Congress is not to prohibit the free exercise of religion. This principle or law was grossly violated when prayer and Bible reading were removed from our schools.

To understand the importance of maintaining a separation between Church and State, one should consider from whence the the first settlers came and why they migrated to this land. For the most part, the early settlers came from Britain. In Britain, the Puritans and Separatists were persecuted by the Anglican Church which was and is the State Church. The people did not enjoy freedom of religion in Britain with the exception of that brief period under Cromwell. Since the head of the Anglican Church is the king, to break with the Anglican Church and seek to establish another form of worship was an act of treason because this action challenged the authority of the king who presided over the Church. The Dissenters, such as the Separatists, were looked upon as traitors when they broke with the Anglican Church. (The Puritans never actually broke with the Church but rather sought to purify it.) Being viewed as traitors, they were thrown into prison and had their goods confiscated.

This led to what was called the "Erastian Controversy." Erastus argued that no congregation had the right to excommunicate anyone from the Church. The king alone had the power to excommunicate and no other. This was an imitation of Rome. The Separatists and Puritans who wanted to maintain a pure fellowship were met with strong opposition, especially when it came to church discipline.

This was no different in some respects in Scotland where the Presbyterian Church was the State Church. They too had a ruling body outside the local assembly. In fact, since Constantine the Great, all the nations of the world have had their State churches, and many saints have been persecuted by them. The saints, such as the Novatians and the Donatists, were persecuted unto death. Later the Waldensees in the Alps and the Huguenots in France suffered the same fate. The Anabaptists were not excluded from such horrors. These poor saints all suffered in the extreme. Therefore, the Founders purposely would not establish a State Church. They did understand that Biblical Christianity undergirded the Republic; therefore, they never made a separation between Christianity and the State. In fact, they vigorously promoted it!

In this light, it is interesting to note that the first Supreme Court Justice, John Jay, was a Huguenot. As a Huguenot, Jay well knew that a State Church could inflict much persecution. It is also worth noting that Jay, along with Henry Laurens and Elias Boudinot, were three Continental Congress presidents who were Huguenots. These men, as well as the Founders, understood the danger of a State

Church. They were descendants of those who had fled from Europe in order to worship God according to their conscience. The nation as a whole understood the imperativeness of not having a State Church. But the nation equally understood the absolute necessity of Christianity.

Alexis de Tocqueville, the famous historian who visited America when James Madison was president, wrote the following:

> In France, I knew the spirit of religion and the spirit of liberty almost always pulled in opposite directions. In the United States I found them intimately interwoven: together they ruled the same territory......My desire to understand the cause of this phenomenon increased with each passing day.

> In order to learn more about this, I questioned the faithful of all communions. I especially sought out the company of clergymen, who are not only the repositories of various beliefs but also a personal interest in their duration. The religion that I professed brought me unto contact with Catholic clergy, and soon developed a close relationship with several of its member. To each of them I expressed my astonishment and revealed my doubts, and I discovered that they differed among themselves only on matters of detail: to a man, they assigned primary credit for the peaceful ascendancy of religion in their country to the complete separation of church and state. I stated without hesitation that during my stay in America I met no one-Not a single clergyman or layman-who did not agree with the statement." Hence it is in this context there was a definite separation between the Church and the State. But when it came to Christianity, it ruled with the state as the two worked together. [32]

There was no Separation between Christianity and the State

The Founding Fathers never intended that there should be a separation between Christianity and the State. On the contrary, the Republic looked to Biblical Christianity to insure her perpetuity. The Founders unanimously understood that the foundation upon which the Republic rested was God's Word. Along with fulfilling his other roles as one of the Founding Fathers, John Jay was also the founder of the American Bible Society. Every family was to have a Bible at home, and all the children were to learn to read so that they could read the Bible.

On this subject, de Tocqueville, who earlier was quoted, throws great light on this matter. He affirms that there was a separation of Church and State, but there was no separation between Christianity and the State. In this vein, he wrote, "In the United States religion not only regulated mores but extends its empire over intelligence as well…Christianity therefore reigns without impediment." [33] In other words, the conscience of the nation was held captive to the Word of God.

Again he wrote, "I am so convinced that Christianity must be maintained at all cost in the new democracies that I would rather chain priest inside their sanctuaries than allow to venture out" [34] He understood that the nation could not stand as a government of the people, by the people, and for the people unless Christianity reigned. It was understood that the preservation of our form of government was absolutely dependent upon Christianity to insure the mores of the nation without which it would collapse. This is why the Bible was and is the most important document of our Republic.

---

[33] (de Tocqueville, *Democracy in America,* 337)
[34] (de Tocqueville, *Democracy in America,* 637)

This is not merely the persuasion of de Tocqueville but of the nation as well. A few quotes of the Founding Fathers will suffice to affirm what de Tocqueville observed.

George Washington said, "True religion affords to government its surest support." [35]

John Adams said, "Religion and virtue are the only foundations... of republicanism and all free governments." [36]

"Our Constitution was made only for a moral and religious people. It is wholly inadequate to the government of any other." [37]

James Madison stated, "Of all the dispositions and habits which lead to political prosperity, religion and morality are indispensable supports."[38]

Dr John Witherspoon said, "God grant that in America true religion and civil liberty may be inseparable and that the unjust attempts to destroy the one, may in the issue tend to the support and establishment of both."[39]

---

[35] David Barton, *The Myth of Separation* (Aledo, TX: WallBuilders, 1993), 146.

[36] Charles Francis Adams, *The works of John Adams, second President of the United States: with a life of the author, notes and illustrations* (Boston: Little, Brown and Company. 1854), Vol.9, 636.

[37] (Adams, *The works of John Adams, second President of the United States: with a life of the author, notes and illustrations,* 636)

[38] (Washington, *George Washington's Farewell Address*)

[39] John Witherspoon, D.D., *The Dominion of Providence Over the Passions of Men. A Sermon, Preached at Princeton, on the 17th of May, 1776. Being The General FAST appointed by the Congress through the United Colonies. To Which is Added, An Address to the Natives of Scotland, Residing in America.* (Philadelphia: Printed, 1777), 38.

Therefore, a government "of the people, by the people, and for the people" is only insured as long as people are able to govern themselves. If the fear of God is ever lost, so goes the nation. In light of this truth, we should be greatly alarmed in what has taken place. Our nation is destroyed and will never recover from her fall unless she returns to the Lord. She must put away the idea of separation of Christianity and the State. This is imperative!

The Warren Court

In the 1960's, the nation made a radical departure in severing herself from her roots. The Warren Court gave a different twist to the term of "separation of Church and State." Their ruling was absurd, as there never was a State Church. The wording of "the separation of Church and State" had now taken on a different meaning. The decision handed down by the Warren Court removed God from the public square. Their ruling undermined the very foundation of the Republic. The removal of prayer and Bible reading from our schools and the striking down of the Sabbath laws was a radical departure from our form of government that was handed down to us from the Founding Fathers. For 187 years, from the declaration of our Independence until 1962, no such rulings were ever made by any court. In fact, the opposite was true. Prior to that time, America was declared a Christian nation by the High Court. The justices of the Warren Court took upon themselves to overrule the previous rulings of the High Court and to reshape the nation.

For example, in the case ***Church of the Holy Trinity v. United States***, **143 U. S. 457 1892, the Court ruled**:

If we pass beyond these matters to a view of American life, as expressed by its laws, its business, its customs, and its society, we find everywhere a clear recognition of the same truth. Among other matters, note the following: the form of oath universally prevailing, concluding with an appeal to the Almighty; the custom of opening sessions of all deliberative bodies and most conventions with prayer; the prefatory words of all wills, "In the name of God, amen"; the laws respecting the observance of the Sabbath, with the general cessation of all secular business, and the closing of courts, legislatures, and other similar public assemblies on that day; the churches and church organizations which abound in every city, town, and hamlet; the multitude of charitable organizations existing everywhere under Christian auspices; the gigantic missionary associations, with general support, and aiming to establish Christian missions in every quarter of the globe. These, and many other matters which might be noticed, add a volume of unofficial declarations to the mass of organic utterances that this is a Christian nation...[40]

The men on the Warren Court were politicians and not justices. Earl Warren was a governor of California for 10 years, appointed to the High Court by President Eisenhower. Hugo Black (1937-1971) was a United States senator for 10 years. He was one of President Roosevelt's appointees to the Court. This was true also of Felix Frankfurter (1939-1962), who was the founder of the ACLU and had previously served as Assistant to the Secretary of Labor.

Then there was Justice William Douglas (1939-1975), Chairman of the Securities and Exchange Commission, a Roosevelt appointee. Justice Tom C. Clark (1949-1967) was the Assistant Attorney General under Presidents Roosevelt and Truman and was later promoted to the Supreme Court by President Truman. Justice William J. Brennan, Jr. (1956-1990), appointed by Eisenhower, was a progressive, influencing the courts more than any other justice in the history of the Court.

---

[40] https://en.wikipedia.org/wiki/Church_of_the_Holy_Trinity_v._United_States

Justice John M. Harlan (1955-1971), Assistant U. S. Attorney for the southern District of New York and Assistant Attorney General of New York, was appointed to the bench by Eisenhower. President Eisenhower also appointed Justice Charles E. Whittaker (1957-1982) to the Supreme Court, moving him up from Associate Justice. He was weak in his rulings as he was more of a swing vote. These eight voted to overthrow the Sabbath laws, ruling a separation of Church and State.

Lastly, Eisenhower appointed Justice Potter Stewart (1958-1981). He previously served as a federal judge before his appointment to the High Court. He was the only one who was not a politician but a true judge. He referred to himself as a lawyer. By that, he meant that he had a respect for the Law. He stood alone against the ruling of removing the Bible out of the schools and striking down the Sabbath laws.

In all, five justices were appointed by Eisenhower, a Republican President. President Truman appointed one justice by elevating a Roosevelt appointee to the High Court, and Roosevelt appointed the rest. All these justices, with the exception of one, were determined to reshape the nation. In doing so, they severed the nation from her roots. As a cut flower, she cannot long survive. In time, she will bow her head and pass away as the other nations had before her. Presently, such signs are evident as the nation is divided. Her strength was the LORD. He was her Protector and Guide. Her Motto was "In God We Trust," but she has forgotten her God and misplaced her trust. This is what happened when she failed to "Remember the Sabbath day, to keep it holy."

The Changing of the Court

There was a radical change that gradually took place in our courts. At one time, laws were to insure domestic tranquility. But from the time of President Woodrow Wilson, there was a gradual mutation that took place. Justices no longer saw themselves as ruling according to law but rather as leaders of social reforms. Gradually and yet definitely, their rulings championed individual rights at the expense of society.

Individual rights were guaranteed by the Constitution; however, now they have been taken beyond the Constitution. Justices' rulings have undermined those laws that insured domestic tranquility. For example, one person was offended because of prayer in school. Hence, the rights of one individual were championed at the expense of the nation. Presently, no one is allowed to pray in public though some still do.

Such rulings have brought on an avalanche of horrors, epitomized in the "human rights" movement where, as in the times of Judges, "every man did that which was right in his own eyes" (Judges 17:6 and 21:25). As a result, we are witnessing every institution crumbling as lawlessness abounds. Times have become so oppressive that our worst enemies are not those from abroad but those living next door to us. We may thank the courts for ruling in favor of individuals at the expense of society. Rights that supersede responsibility breed anarchy!

The Declension of the Nation

It is difficult for us standing in the 21st century to perceive just how far we have fallen. Gatto states something in his book, *A Different Kind of Teacher*, that was altogether arresting.[41] He pointed out that 70 percent of all the lawyers in the entire world reside in the United States. This figure in itself is astonishing. But it becomes even more pronounced when we consider that we, in these United States of

---

[41] John Taylor Gatto, *A different Kind of Teacher* (Berkeley CA: Berkeley Hill Books, 2001), 186-187.

America, make up less than 7 percent of the world population. Is this not telling?

What does this statistic say about the character of our nation? Or better still, what does this have to say about you and me? Certainly, we cannot escape the fact that a handshake is meaningless, oaths are vain, and contracts are useless. How have we fallen into such a deplorable condition? Can it be that we have no fear of God before our eyes?

The Sabbath and Economics

With the loss of the Sabbath observance, there is also the loss of a consciousness of God. The nation has imperceptibly departed from the Lord, especially with the striking down of the Sabbath laws. But even before these laws were changed, there was the gradual loss of the Protestant work ethic which made America the most prosperous nation in the world. Adam Smith's Laissez-faire economic philosophy has been set to naught as Keynesian economics lifted its ugly head. With the Great Depression, President Roosevelt thought it necessary for the government to intervene in the economics of the nation. This was the position of John Stuart Mills as well as John Maynard Keynes. However, with government intervention, the Depression lasted much longer than if it had been left to run its course.

Presently with the government regulating the economy, liberation theology has now been brought into play. This is nothing new as this doctrine was first set forth by Thomas Aquinas. Thomas Aquinas rejected personal ownership of property. His position was that all things are for the common good. Therefore, the "have nots" may steal and loot since all goods are common. If people steal or loot, they are just taking what is rightfully theirs. To loot or to steal is not a crime nor is it a sin. This is the theology of South America and Roman Catholic countries as well.

President Johnson's "Great Society" was nothing more than the implementation of liberation theology which President Roosevelt introduced. His objective was to do away with poverty and social injustice. He taxed the rich to give to the poor. However, both poverty and crime increased. In turn, the wealth of the nation had greatly decreased, and crime escalated. Notwithstanding, this is the course the nation adamantly pursues. Presently, a job applicant's qualifications do not matter as much as quotas that must be filled. Why? Wealth must be redistributed for the common good of all.

President Obama was greatly imbued with liberation theology. This was the teaching of his pastor, Reverend Wright, under whom he sat for many years. Is it any wonder that President Obama gave Chrysler Corporation to a union that belonged to stock holders who in turn sold it to Germany? Another example of liberation theology is "Obama Care." These are just a few examples of how liberation theology has infiltrated even the highest places in our government.

On the other hand, people who have never worked file tax returns to receive their share of the common goods. The welfare programs implemented are nothing more than the redistribution of wealth. The rich are heavily taxed to give to the poor. Is it any wonder that many businesses left the country under President Obama? President Trump brought many companies back by simply lifting the tax burden. In doing so, he also created more jobs. So much for this liberation theology!

When we fail to observe the Sabbath, we lose consciousness of God and the Protestant work ethic. The Protestant work ethic is to work and not look for handouts. In 2 Thessalonians 3:10, we read, "For even when we were with you, this we commanded you, that if any would not work, neither should he eat." At the same time we are admonished to work so that we might have to give to the needy (Ephesians 4:28). Hospitals, orphanages, and the like were at one time funded and operated by Christians and not by the government or private businesses. With the loss of the Sabbath, we have forgotten our duty to God and man, and with that, we ceased to be responsible, thus forgoing our liberties.

The Church

The church is the light of the world and the salt of the earth. She is the only light in this world and the only means of staying corruption. She is to be a shining light dispelling darkness, but she has failed to fulfill her calling because she has lost her light as well as her savor. Presently, both pastors and people alike profane the Sabbath without the least sting of conscience. This has lead to other flagrant sins because the conscience has been seared. Those who seek to hallow the Sabbath are looked upon as extremists. This viewpoint is not held so much by the world as it is by professing Christians. This is how far we have departed from the Lord.

Presently, the Church is caught up in politics. Church members vigorously campaign for their favorite candidates. Such organizations as the Moral Majority and the Christian Coalition are two examples of how the Church is seeking to influence and reform our government. But how is she expected to reform the government without first reforming herself? The above endeavors are failures because the Church is corrupt. Worse still, she has been sanctifying that which is abominable. Have we not read, "For the time is come that judgment must begin at the house of God: and if it first *begin* at us, what shall the end be of them that obey not the gospel of God?" (1 Peter 4:17). (emphasis added)

If we are to influence the world and if we are to stem the tide, then we must repent. The problem is not with the world but with the Church. The world has always been corrupt, so it is the church's responsibility to stay the corruption. This is the only means God provided. The church at one time had a powerful influence upon government. Of the early Church it was said, "...these that have turned the world upside down are come hither also" (Acts 17:6). Such events are unheard of today. Why? If God has not changed, then the problem must rest with us!

Let us then pause and examine ourselves. Our Lord has commanded the Church to preach repentance and faith in His name. He had never changed the means by which nations are to be brought into the light. When people are changed, then the nation is changed. Light dispels darkness. We must keep in mind that the nation is made up of people like you and me. Without question there must be a revival. It must start at the grass roots before there will be a reviving in Washington. We had two great revivals in our country. Nothing less than another great awakening will turn the nation back to God and stay His wrath. But we must first heed the call to return to the Lord. We must begin by ceasing to profane the Sabbath. This is the proper place to begin. We must seek the Lord with all of our heart. Then He will hear from heaven.

Have we strayed so far away
That God's wrath cannot be stayed?
Have we spurned His loving call
Will we as a nation fall?

I know not what others do.
The question is what will you do?
As for me, I'll seek His Face,
And cling to His unchanging Grace.

BIBLIOGRAPHY

Adams, Charles Francis. *The works of John Adams, second President of the United States: with a life of the author, notes and illustrations.* Boston: Little, Brown and Company. 1854. Vol. 9.

Barton, David. *The Myth of Separation.* Aledo, TX: WallBuilders, 1993.

Blakely, William Addison. *American State Papers Bearing on Sunday Legislation.* Washington D.C.: The Religious Liberty Association, 1911.

De Tocqueville, Alexis. *Democracy in America.* New York: The Library of America, 2004.

Farris, Michael. *The History of Religious Liberty.* Green Forest, AR: Master Books, 2015.

Gatto, John Taylor. *A Different Kind of Teacher.* Berkeley: Berkeley Hill Books, 2001.

Griffith, William O. *John Bunyan.* London: Hodder and Stoughton, 1927.

Josephus, F. *The Complete Works of Josephus.* Grand Rapids: Kregel, 1981.

Keyes, Nelson Beecher. *Ben Franklin: An Affectionate Portrait.*

Garden City, NY: Hanover House, 1956.

Murphy, Paul. *The Constitution in Crisis Times 1918-1969.*

New York, San Francisco, London: Harper & Row. 1972.

Nietzsche, Friedrich. *Search for the meaning of life.*

NY, Chicago, San Francisco: Holt, Rinehart & Winston. 1962.

Sayce, Archibald H. *Social Life Among the Assyrians and Babylonians.* New York: Fleming H. Revel Co. 1893.

Smith, George. *Assyrian Discoveries.* New York: Scribner, Armstrong & Co, 1875.

"Shabbat Elevator." *Wikipedia.org.* 13 May 2018. Web 8 June 2018.

Theophilus. "To Autolycus." Trans. Marcus Dods. *The Ante-Nicene Fathers.* New York: Charles Scribner's Son, 1913. Vol. 2.

Trench, Richard Chenevix. *Synonyms of the New Testament.*

Grand Rapids: Associated Publishers and Authors Inc.

Washington, George. *George Washington's Farewell Address.*

Belford, MA: Applewood Books, 1993.

Winthrop, Robert C. *Addresses and Speeches on Various Occasions.* Boston: Little, Brown, and Company, 1852.

Witherspoon, John D.D.. *The Dominion of Providence Over the Passions of Men. A Sermon, Preached at Princeton, on the 17ᵗʰ of May, 1776. Being The General FAST appointed by the Congress through the United Colonies. To Which is Added, An Address to the Natives of Scotland, Residing in America.* Philadelphia: Printed, 1777.

http://Wikinpedia.org

https://en.wikipedia.org/wiki/Church_of_the_Holy_Trinity_v._United_States

http://providencefoundation.com/?page_id=888

https://en.wikipedia.org/wiki/History_of_Princeton_University

ABOUT THE AUTHOR

C. H. Pappas was born in Washington D. C. of parents who migrated from Greece. Up until the fifth grade, he found himself wandering. His father was gone, and his mother who could not speak English raised the family of four girls and one boy without government assistance. When he was in fifth grade, his teacher, Mrs. Nesbit, awakened his soul by introducing to him the Founding Fathers. Being greatly moved by their example, they soon became his heroes. Their virtue and sacrifice so impressed him that he eagerly began reading their biographies. One evening walking home after school, his eyes swelled up with tears of gratitude that God had so ordained that he should be born in America!

After finishing the eleventh grade, he joined the U.S. Marine Corp. Unlike his peers, he was a moral and devout Greek Orthodox. After serving in the Marine Corp, he worked as a carpenter. His goal was to be a contractor. It was during this period of his life that the Lord revealed his heart to him. For the first time he saw his utter vileness. The good works, which he hoped would secure eternal life, were those that weighed the heaviest upon him. He found himself hopelessly damned before a holy and just God. Under horrible conviction, he knew not what to do.

Being greatly troubled, he went to a neighboring Catholic Church to pray. As he walked up to the Church, he saw two priests were standing on the steps talking. Approaching them he asked, "Father, are you going to heaven?" They laughed and said, "No one knows that until he dies." Then he asked, "What does it mean to be born again?" They smiled and said, "You need not bother yourself with that." Immediately, he knew something was wrong because Jesus said, "Ye must be born again." He knew that they could not help him; they did not know where they were going. He then entered the Church and began to pray crying out to God for mercy. With no one did he dare share the agonizing burden of his heart. He cried, "Is there any hope for one such as I?"

Then one day shortly thereafter his son, who was five years old at the time, approached him asking, "Daddy, will you help me learn this verse?" The verse was John 3:16. He had never heard that passage in his entire life. As he taught his son, he also memorized the passage.

The next day as he was working, John 3:16 kept rolling over and over in his mind. He thought, "Yes, God must love the world, He gave His only begotten Son. I could never do that. Yes, God no doubt loves the world—but God cannot love me. I am too vile." Over and over this singular thought seized his mind until the words "whosoever believeth in Him should not perish but have everlasting life" gripped his soul. He stopped. He was arrested. He thought, "Surely 'whosoever' means me! Can it be that God loves me?" He then cried, "Lord, I do believe on Thee!" Immediately, the burden rolled away. Resting now upon the promise of God Who cannot lie, he felt a peace, as never before experienced, flood his soul. The world that was draped in black suddenly broke into splendid light!

In awe, not able to fully grasp all that was said in that sublime passage, he wandered for several days asking, "Can it be God really loves me?" The very thought was staggering! Then one day, his wife asked, "Are you saved?" To this he replied, "I am not saved by what I have done but solely by the grace of God." There was no boasting but humble adoration for God Who so loves the world. The following Lord's Day he attended Palm Springs North Baptist Church and made a public confession of faith. The following week, he was baptized, and the week thereafter, he was called to preach. This alarmed him as he saw himself so unfit for such a task. But the call weighed heavily upon him, and he finally surrendered. Upon his pastor's recommendation, he immediately enrolled in Miami Dade Junior College and finished his work at Florida Junior College where he received his Associate of Arts degree. He also attended Luther Rice Seminary where he received both his Bachelors of Divinity and his Masters in Theology. He completed six years of work in a little over three years, graduating with honors.

While in school, he worked supporting his family and preaching in the city rescue mission. He taught and preached in the churches as well. Upon graduating, he taught the doctrine of the atonement at Luther Rice Seminary. After leaving there, he taught Bible through an extension course of Florida Junior College. Though he was met with opposition, he continued to teach, leading the class from Genesis through Revelation. The Lord blessed his labors as He saved some, strengthened others, and called still others to fulltime mission work. He also pastored at Bible Baptist Church.

In 1978, Chris Pappas was called to Collins Road Baptist Church which had just started a Christian school for Kindergarten through twelfth grade students. He accepted the call, and the two churches merged. He presently pastors his flock at Collins Road Baptist Church where he has served for forty years.

Chris Pappas is married and has three sons, eight grandchildren, and eight great grandchildren. He has authored another book, *In Defense of the Authenticity of 1 John 5:7*. This book on the Sabbath is the second book he has published, and he is presently working on a third. He is consumed by the love of God and for the flock God has placed under his care. Having a burden for the saints and a jealousy for God, he has taken up his pen to strengthen and encourage the saints in these days of utter darkness.

Printed in the United States
By Bookmasters